ReThink Nonprofits

A New Approach to Making a Difference

By Jordan Patrick
Founder & CEO of RaiseMore

Foreword

In the nonprofit world, we're often told that certain rules are inviolable. We're conditioned to think that because our currency is change, not profit, the same aggressive strategies that transform industries don't apply to us. We're led to believe that passion will fill the gaps where pragmatic tactics should be.

This book challenges those preconceptions. It's built on the premise that nonprofits can learn a great deal from startup culture. This isn't about rejecting the ethos of nonprofit work; it's about refining it, injecting a dose of realism, and preparing your organization to make a genuine, lasting impact.

Inspired by the book "Rework," this is a compass for the modern nonprofit, pointing towards methods that are as effective as they are ethical. These pages are a manifesto for change-makers who are not afraid to question the status quo and rewrite the rules for a noble cause. Every chapter is an invitation to rethink, retool, and revitalize the way you run your nonprofit.

We'll traverse the terrain of debunking myths, igniting beginnings, strategizing movements, enhancing effectiveness, embracing community, and upholding values. This is not about mimicking the startup hustle in a way that burns you out. It's about adopting a mindset that prioritizes smart work, sustainable growth, and, most importantly, the mission that set you in motion.

You're holding a handbook for the audacious — the nonprofit leaders, volunteers, and visionaries who are ready to rethink the typical Nonprofit approach for greater impact. Let's begin.

Introduction
Rewriting the Nonprofit Playbook

Welcome to a journey that defies the conventional. If you're holding this book, chances are you're involved with a nonprofit or are working in the industry of social change. Whether you're a seasoned leader with many campaigns under your belt or a fiery newcomer eager to make your mark, this book is for you.

But please be warned, this isn't your typical nonprofit handbook.

The world we live in is rapidly changing, and the landscape of social good is evolving with it. The strategies that worked yesterday might not work today, and the practices of today might be obsolete tomorrow. To make a real impact, to change lives, and to advance your cause, you need to think differently. You need to work smarter, not just harder.

In the spirit of "Rework" — the revolutionary business book that turned the corporate world on its head—we will break down outdated notions that have long clung to the fabric of nonprofit work. We will challenge the myths that restrain us, deconstruct the assumptions that hold us back, and reconstruct a framework that empowers nonprofits to act with the agility and innovation of the most dynamic startups.

Throughout this book, each chapter will confront a different piece of conventional nonprofit wisdom, inviting you to look at it from a fresh perspective. We'll discuss why "Nonprofits can't be innovative" is not just a myth but a misjudgment of the sector's potential. We'll explore the power of starting with what you have, embracing constraints, and fostering a culture that prioritizes mission over bureaucracy.

This is an invitation to adopt a mindset of growth and resilience, to embrace the lessons of failure and the clarity of simplicity. It's a call to distill your efforts to their most potent form, ensuring every action and decision aligns with the ultimate goal: making a sustainable impact.

As we move forward, remember that each chapter, each idea, is a piece of a larger puzzle. You won't find long-winded theories or complex models here—only straightforward, actionable insights that you can apply immediately. It's a guide designed for the trenches of nonprofit work, where time is precious and results matter.

So, let's begin. Turn the page, and let's rewrite the nonprofit playbook together. Your passion and your mission deserve no less.

Table of Contents

Part 1 - Myths Debunked
3. "Nonprofits Can't Be Innovative" is a Myth
5. Learning From What Works
7. Strategic Guesses Over Detailed Plans
9. Scale the impact, Not Just Size
11. Purposeful Work, Not Burnout
13. The Myth of the Typical Nonprofit

Part 2 - Beginnings
16. Make Your Cause Resonate
18. Solve Real Problems
20. Get Started with What You Have
22. There's Always Time to Make a Difference
24. Define your Impact
26. Mission Statements That Mean Something
28. Grants Aren't the Only Way
30. Do More with the Right Less
32. Build Movements, Not Organizations
34. Sustainable Impact over Quick Exits
36. Stay Agile and Adaptable

Part 3 - Making Moves
39. Constraints Foster Creativity
41. Quality Over Quantity in Service
43. Focus on the Core Mission
45. Big Visions Start with Small Details
47. Decisive Action Moves Missions Forward
49. Curate Your Initiatives
51. Less Noise, More Signal
53. Embrace Enduring Values
55. The Integrity of Your Mission
57. Repurpose to Amplify Your Impact
59. It's a Marathon, Not a Sprint

Part 4 - Competition
62. Collaboration Over Competition
64. Embrace Your Community's Growth
66. Prioritize with Your Mission
68. Ground-level Excellence

70. The Paper Trail Can Wait

Part 5 - Outreach
73. The Power of Being Lesser-Known
75. Cultivate Your Community
77. Teach as You Learn
79. Share Your Recipes for Change
81. The Impact of Transparency
83. Authenticity Over Aesthetics

Part 6 - Team Building
86. Recruit for Necessity, Not Luxury
88. Chapter 1: The Right Person, Not Just Any Person
90. Diverse Teams, Richer Solutions
92. The Fallacy of the Perfect Resume
94. Experience Beyond Years
96. Look Beyond Credentials

Part 7 - Resilience
99. When Things Go Wrong, Own It
101. The Speed of Response Matters
103. The Art of the Genuine Apology
105. Frontline Empathy
107. Take a Breath Before Responding

Part 8 - Values
110. Culture is Lived, Not Imposed
112. Fluid Decisions for a Stable Mission
114. Beyond Rock Stars and Heroes
116. Respect is Non-Negotiable
118. Encourage Life Beyond Work
120. First Mistakes Aren't Failures
122. Cut the Jargon
124. Urgency Must Be Warranted
126. Authentic Voice
128. Begin with the Mission in Mind

Conclusion
130. Forging Ahead

Part 1
Myths Debunked

Chapter 1
"Nonprofits Can't be Innovative" is a Myth

In the nonprofit realm, we often romanticize innovation, equating it with invention. We chase after the allure of being the first, the pioneer. Yet, true innovation isn't always about crafting something from nothing—it's just as often about observing, adapting, and applying what works.

Innovation in nonprofits is not only possible; it's happening. It's in the creative ways organizations stretch budgets further than they should logically go. It's in the groundbreaking approaches to solving systemic problems that have baffled for-profit sectors for years. And it's in the tireless pursuit of mission over margin, where the real measure of success is not in wealth accumulated, but in lives changed.

The truth is, innovation is not about the resources you have; it's about the mindset you cultivate. It's the volunteer who devises a more efficient way to distribute resources. It's the fundraiser who thinks of a new platform to gather donations. It's the marketer who tells your story in a way that catches the public's imagination and refuses to let go.

Nonprofits can—and do—embrace risk. They try new things, fail fast, and adapt quicker than many sclerotic corporate giants. They have to. When your currency is change, stagnation is the enemy, and bold moves are the allies of progress.

The next time you hear someone say, "Nonprofits can't be innovative," take it as a challenge. Innovate in how you engage with your community. Be groundbreaking in your transparency. Be inventive in your collaborations. Rework the very idea of what a nonprofit can be.

Reject the myth. Embrace the truth. Your cause depends on it.

Chapter 2
Learning From What Works

In the nonprofit realm, we often romanticize innovation, equating it with invention. We chase after the allure of being the first, the pioneer. Yet, true innovation isn't always about crafting something from nothing—it's just as often about observing, adapting, and applying what works.

We see successful strategies deployed by others—perhaps a campaign that went viral or a funding model that's sustaining growth. Instead of nodding appreciatively and moving on, we should ask, "How can this work for us?" Learning from what works doesn't mean you copy-paste a model indiscriminately. It means you analyze its essence, adapt its strengths, and avoid its pitfalls.

Nonprofits have a treasure trove of case studies, from decades of collective experience. It's a rich soil where the seeds of proven strategies can grow. But the trick lies in not just transplanting them into your organization. Instead, cultivate them. Cross-pollinate ideas from different fields, different causes, different sizes of organizations.

Look around. Is there a local nonprofit engaging with the community in transformative ways? How are international NGOs leveraging technology for global change? What can you learn from the startup next door about agility and scaling impact?

Every success story is a learning opportunity. Every misstep, a lesson in what to avoid. This isn't about losing your originality; it's about smart innovation—rooted in the wisdom of the past and the realities of the present, blossoming into strategies that carry your unique mission forward.

Learning from what works is a shortcut to effectiveness. It's not the easy road; it's the smart one. And for nonprofits stretched thin on resources but rich in determination, it may just be the most innovative approach of all.

Chapter 3
Strategic Guesses Over Detailed Plans

The traditional model for nonprofits has long touted the need for comprehensive, detailed plans. The assumption is that with enough contingencies considered, a plan can be foolproof. But the world changes too fast for such meticulousness to guarantee success. Instead, successful nonprofits are learning to lean into strategic guesses—thoughtful assumptions that allow for flexibility and quick pivots.

Think of a strategic guess as your organization's hypothesis. It's informed, it's intelligent, but it's not immovable. When you make a strategic guess, you're accepting that you can't predict everything. What you can do is identify your north star and chart a course towards it, knowing full well that the winds might change and you'll need to adjust your sails.

It's like planning a route in unfamiliar territory. A detailed plan would have you plot every turn, every stop, every contingency for traffic. But a strategic guess recognizes the goal is to reach the destination, not to follow the plan to the letter. If there's a roadblock, you adapt. If there's a shortcut, you take it. It's this adaptability that often separates thriving nonprofits from those that struggle.

This isn't advocating for recklessness. Each guess should be grounded in data, in experience, in the collective wisdom of your team. But it also means embracing uncertainty. When a fundraiser doesn't pan out, or a campaign isn't as successful as anticipated, your mission isn't derailed because your plan was never about rigid adherence to a set path.

Strategic guesses empower nonprofits to move with the kind of agility typically reserved for startups. They free you from the paralysis of planning and open up the possibilities of what you can achieve when you're not bound to what you thought would work.

So, as you look ahead, plan less for precision, and more for potential. The goal isn't to predict the future; it's to prepare to meet it, however it unfolds.

Chapter 4
Scale the Impact, Not Just Size

In the nonprofit sector, success isn't measured by scale in the traditional sense. It's not about how big your office is, how many people you employ, or even how many branches you have worldwide. It's about the scale of your impact – the depth and breadth of the difference you're making in the world.

The pursuit of scaling up can be a siren song that leads nonprofits away from their core missions. The pressure to grow can result in a diluted purpose and a strained infrastructure. Instead, consider scaling your impact. This means honing in on what you do best and finding ways to do it even better, for more people, more effectively.

Scaling impact is a mindful approach to growth. It means ensuring that every new step you take – whether it's a new program, partnership, or market – is mission-aligned and amplifying the change you're making. It's about leveraging your strengths and making calculated moves that multiply your effectiveness without compromising your values.

Ask yourself: if your organization doubled in size but didn't increase its effectiveness, would that be success? True growth for a nonprofit is found in the smiles of those you help, the communities you empower, and the environments you safeguard.

To scale impact, start small. Test new ideas on a micro-scale before rolling them out. Listen to feedback, from both the communities you serve and your team. And remember, sometimes the most powerful way to scale isn't by expanding your organization, but by empowering others, sharing your knowledge, and collaborating for greater reach.

Impact is the true scale of change. Focus on that, and your organization will grow in the ways that truly matter.

Chapter 5
Purposeful Work, Not Burnout

Nonprofit work is often driven by a passion for the cause. Yet, there's a shadow that looms over many mission-driven organizations—burnout. It's a product of long hours, emotional labor, and the persistent feeling that the work is never done. To change this narrative, nonprofits must pivot towards creating environments of purposeful work that energize rather than exhaust.

Purposeful work is about alignment—aligning tasks with talents, goals with roles, and individual purpose with organizational mission. It's about knowing that the hours spent working translate directly into the impact made. This alignment creates a natural efficiency that not only propels the mission forward but also sustains the people behind it.

Combatting burnout isn't about adding more downtime—it's about making the work itself more fulfilling. It involves setting clear boundaries that honor the individual's need for rest and rejuvenation. It means saying no to the culture of overwork and yes to focused, intentional efforts.

Nonprofits must embrace the idea that busy isn't the same as productive. A team member staring at a computer screen late into the night isn't a badge of honor; it's a sign that something in the system is broken. Productivity should be measured in outcomes, not hours. The focus should be on achieving milestones that push the mission forward, not on filling timesheets.

Leaders in the nonprofit sector have the responsibility to set the tone. They can do this by showcasing their commitment to purposeful work and balance. This means leaving the office on time, encouraging breaks, and prioritizing well-being. When leadership models this behavior, it sets a precedent, creating a ripple effect throughout the organization.

Purposeful work leads to fulfillment, not fatigue. It energizes teams, fuels passion, and sparks creativity. It's the antidote to burnout and the key to sustainable success in the nonprofit world.

Chapter 6
The Myth of the Typical Nonprofit

There's a common misconception that nonprofits are cut from the same cloth, sharing the same structures, challenges, and goals. This "typical" nonprofit is often seen as underfunded, understaffed, and operating on the edge of survival. However, this image fails to capture the vast diversity and the dynamic nature of the sector.

The nonprofit world is not monolithic; it's a tapestry. From grassroots movements to international NGOs, from art collectives to research institutions, nonprofits embody a multitude of missions, cultures, and methodologies. The needs of a local food bank differ vastly from those of a global health charity, just as the resources available to a large foundation are not the same as those for a community advocacy group.

Embracing this diversity is crucial. The strategies that propel one organization to success may not be applicable or appropriate for another. Best practices are not one-size-fits-all; they must be adapted to fit the unique context of each organization.

Furthermore, the narrative that nonprofits must scrape by reinforces harmful stereotypes that can limit potential. It creates a scarcity mindset that stifles innovation and ambition. While it's true that resources are often tight, it's also true that nonprofits are remarkably resourceful, capable of achieving impressive outcomes with limited means.

The "typical" nonprofit myth can also overshadow the professionalism and expertise found within the sector. Nonprofits are not just passion projects; they are professional enterprises requiring a diverse range of skills and talents. From fundraising and management to research and advocacy, nonprofit work demands a high level of sophistication and strategy.

Breaking down this myth means recognizing that there is no

single story of nonprofit operation. Each organization must be understood on its own terms, with its own set of strengths, challenges, and opportunities. It's in this nuanced understanding that the sector can begin to move away from limiting stereotypes and toward a more accurate appreciation of its dynamic nature.

Part 2
Beginnings

Chapter 7
Make Your Cause Resonate

In the cacophony of calls to action, urgent appeals, and the clamor for attention, how does a nonprofit make its cause resonate? It's not just about having a compelling mission; it's about connecting that mission to the people you're trying to reach in a way that strikes a chord.

The heart of resonance lies in storytelling. A well-told story can turn statistics into personal narratives, beneficiaries into protagonists, and abstract goals into concrete visions of a better world. The most resonant stories are those that are authentic, relatable, and evoke emotion. They don't just inform; they inspire and engage.

Your cause becomes resonant when it's seen as more than just a good idea—it's perceived as a movement that individuals want to be part of. It's about framing your mission in a way that intersects with your audience's values, experiences, and aspirations. When people see their own reflections in your work, the cause becomes theirs, too.

Resonance also comes from clarity. In a landscape of complex challenges and nuanced missions, the ability to distill your message to its essence is vital. People should be able to understand not only what you do but why it matters, with just a glance or a few words. The clearer your message, the further it will travel.

Don't shy away from leveraging emotion. While the intellect understands the need for change, it's the heart that commits to it. Emotionally charged messages can be a powerful catalyst for action. However, balance is key—overusing pathos can lead to message fatigue. Aim for a message that motivates rather than manipulates.

Finally, make your cause resonate by making it tangible. Show the impact of a donation, the change that volunteering brings, or the difference that advocacy can make. People resonate with what they can see, touch, and understand. The more tangible the impact, the more compelling the cause.

Making your cause resonate is about finding the intersection of storytelling, clarity, emotion, and tangibility. It's where the frequency of your mission's message matches the wavelength of your audience's heart and mind.

Chapter 8
Solve Real Problems

In the world of nonprofits, the impetus to solve real problems should be the cornerstone of every initiative. The success of a nonprofit is not in the grandeur of its mission statement but in its capacity to address tangible issues that affect real people's lives.

At the heart of solving real problems is the art of listening. Before jumping to solutions, the most effective nonprofits take time to understand the nuances of the challenges they aim to address. They listen to the communities they serve, recognizing them not just as beneficiaries but as partners with valuable insights. This collaborative approach ensures that solutions are not just applied but are co-created.

Solving real problems means focusing on impact over intentions. Good intentions can pave the way for action, but they do not guarantee results. It's the outcomes that matter—the measurable changes that make a difference in the community. Nonprofits need to be rigorous in assessing their impact, willing to pivot when a strategy isn't working, and transparent about both successes and failures.

Innovation is another key component. Traditional methods may have their place, but solving modern problems often requires innovative thinking. This doesn't necessarily mean adopting the latest technology; it means finding creative, sustainable solutions that can be implemented effectively, even on a tight budget.

Nonprofits also have the responsibility to educate. By raising awareness of the problems they're tackling, they can galvanize public support and action. Education empowers communities, equipping them with the knowledge to understand the issues and the tools to address them independently over time.

Moreover, solving real problems is about prioritizing. Nonprofits are often faced with a myriad of issues they wish to confront, but resources are limited. Making tough choices about where to focus energy and resources is crucial. It's often more effective to solve a few problems well than to tackle many with half measures.

To solve real problems, nonprofits must be nimble, responsive, and driven by the real-world impact. It's not just about having a mission; it's about fulfilling that mission through practical, effective, and community-driven solutions that create lasting change.

Chapter 9
Get Started with What You Have

The lore of perfect beginnings can paralyze even the most passionate teams. The truth for nonprofits is that there's never a 'perfect' time to start, nor is there ever a complete set of resources just waiting to be used. The key is to start with what you have.

Beginning with the assets at hand—even if they seem meager—turns the focus towards action rather than waiting. It's about embracing a mentality that combines resourcefulness with resilience. This philosophy holds that the most important step isn't the grand opening, but the small, determined steps taken each day towards progress.

For many nonprofits, the initial resources are often the founders' passion and the problem they want to solve. Begin there. The first version of your program doesn't need to be flawless; it needs to be functional. It's more important to get your services to those in need than to wait for the perfect strategy or the ideal funding.

This 'start where you are' approach also encourages a culture of innovation. Constraints can often be the mother of invention, leading to creative solutions that might not have been considered in a situation of abundance. Nonprofits have found novel ways to use social media, volunteer skills, and community partnerships, turning limitations into launchpads.

What you have is more than possessions or funds; it's the network, the expertise of your team, the knowledge of the community, and the ability to mobilize resources in ways that amplify your impact. Small nonprofits have turned modest beginnings into massive movements by leveraging the power of community and the drive to make a difference.

Getting started with what you have is also an exercise in trust. Trust that your mission will resonate, that your community will respond, and that the support you need will come as you build momentum. This isn't blind faith; it's strategic optimism based on the belief that action begets opportunity.

Starting isn't just a step; it's a statement. It declares that your cause won't wait for conditions to be right or for resources to be ample. It states that change is urgent, necessary, and possible—right now, with what you have.

Chapter 10
There's Always Time to Make a Difference

The clock is often seen as a nemesis in the quest to change the world. There's a misconception that significant contributions require large swathes of uninterrupted time. But the reality in the nonprofit realm is that every second counts, and there's always time to make a difference.

One of the most empowering shifts a nonprofit can make is away from the narrative of scarcity—there's not enough time—to one of abundance—every moment holds potential. It's about seeing the gaps in a schedule not as too insignificant for impact, but as opportunities ripe for meaningful action.

Micro-volunteering is a perfect illustration of this. It breaks down tasks into small, manageable actions that can fit into the briefest of time slots. Whether it's proofreading a document, making a quick phone call to a donor, or sharing a social media post, these acts, though small in time commitment, can accumulate to create substantial impact.

For those leading and working within nonprofits, it's also about redefining productivity. Time spent thinking, planning, or reflecting is not wasted—it's part of the fabric of effective action. Innovation doesn't always come from doing more; sometimes, it comes from thinking differently about what we already do.

This perspective requires a shift in how we measure contribution. The focus moves from the quantity of time spent to the quality of the impact achieved. Nonprofits thrive when they value the short bursts of creativity, the quick decisions, and the ability to adapt plans on the fly just as much as they do the long-term strategies and dedicated projects.

In the same vein, nonprofit leaders must recognize and celebrate the various ways people contribute their time. From the board member who strategizes over lunch breaks to the student who organizes a fundraiser between classes—every moment given is a testament to the collective drive for change.

In essence, time should be seen not as a barrier but as a versatile resource. Nonprofits can craft campaigns that allow anyone to contribute, no matter how limited their schedule may seem. This inclusive approach not only broadens the scope of who can be involved but also enriches the organization with a diversity of input and engagement.

Remember, time is not just a resource to be managed, but a canvas on which to paint acts of change. There's always time to make a difference, and in the world of nonprofits, every second spent towards a cause is a step towards a better world.

Chapter 11
Define your Impact

In the nonprofit sector, success is not measured by profit margins or sales figures, but by the elusive concept of 'impact'. Defining this impact is both an art and a science—it's what frames your narrative, guides your efforts, and, ultimately, tells you whether you're making the difference you set out to make.

The first step to defining your impact is to understand the change you wish to see. This vision must be clear and compelling; it should articulate not only the what but the why. Your definition should resonate with the core of your mission, be it serving a community, protecting the environment, or advocating for a cause.

Once the vision is set, the next challenge is to operationalize it—to break it down into measurable outcomes. This process demands an understanding of indicators that can reliably reflect progress. For an education nonprofit, this could mean literacy rates or graduation numbers. For a health initiative, it might be the reduction in disease incidence or improved access to care.

The key to effective impact measurement is specificity. "Making the world a better place" is a noble goal, but it's too vague to guide action or to assess progress. Instead, your impact should be quantifiable. How many people will you reach? What tangible changes will you bring about in their lives? How will the community or environment be different?

Remember, though, that numbers don't tell the whole story. Qualitative data—stories, testimonials, and case studies—are equally important in painting a full picture of your impact. They provide context to the numbers, turning statistics into narratives that captivate and motivate.

Defining your impact also means setting benchmarks for success.

These should be ambitious enough to drive progress, yet realistic enough to be attainable. And as circumstances change, be prepared to revisit and revise your definitions. Flexibility is not an indication of failure; it's a hallmark of responsiveness and evolution.

Finally, transparency in how you define and measure impact builds trust. Share your successes and your lessons learned. Let your donors, volunteers, and the communities you serve see the roadmap of your impact. This transparency not only fosters trust but also invites collaboration and support.

Defining your impact is a foundational practice for nonprofits. It shapes strategies, inspires stakeholders, and, most importantly, ensures that every effort made is a stride toward the change you aspire to create.

Chapter 12
Mission Statements That Mean Something

A mission statement is the guiding star of a nonprofit organization—it declares purpose, directs strategy, and communicates essence. But a mission statement that is a mere collection of buzzwords strung together, no matter how lofty, serves no one. It must be a clear, concise, and compelling declaration of your organization's raison d'être, its reason for existing.

For a mission statement to mean something, it has to say something—to stir the heart as much as it informs the mind. It needs to be specific enough to differentiate your organization from others, yet broad enough to encompass all that you do. It's not just what you stand for; it's the change you're actively working to create in the world.

To craft such a mission statement, start with the 'why'. Why does your organization exist? This is not about what you do, but the reason behind it—the problem you're solving or the value you're adding to the community or cause. It could be 'empowering underserved youth with education' or 'preserving our region's natural habitats for future generations'.

The next step is to embed your approach or methodology. This is the 'how'. If your mission is to empower youth, how do you do it? Through mentorship programs, by providing scholarships, or by creating safe spaces for learning? This gives a clearer picture of your organization's strategy and operations.

Then, consider the 'who'. Who benefits from your work? Be as specific as possible. 'Underserved youth' can be narrowed down to 'at-risk high school students in urban areas', for instance. This specificity not only makes your mission statement more meaningful but also more memorable.

Remember, your mission statement isn't just internal jargon—it's a tool for engagement. When well-crafted, it can inspire staff, attract volunteers, and resonate with donors. It becomes a message that is easily communicated and widely understood, creating a strong and shared sense of purpose.

A mission statement should also be timeless. While your strategies and objectives may evolve, your mission should remain constant, anchoring your organization through growth and change.

Finally, make it visible. Don't let it gather dust in a business plan or be buried on a website. Embed it in every aspect of your organization—from the language used in fundraising appeals to the way you report on your impact. Let it be the first thing people know about you and the last thing they remember.

Chapter 13
Grants Aren't the Only Way

It's a common belief in the nonprofit world that grants are the lifeblood of charitable organizations. While grants can be a significant source of funding, they are far from the only way to keep your mission moving forward. In fact, over-reliance on grants can lead to a precarious financial situation. The key to sustainability lies in diversifying your revenue streams.

The first step away from grant dependency is to look at what you have to offer. Nonprofits are often treasure troves of value with their networks, knowledge, and social capital. Can you offer consulting services based on your expertise? What about educational workshops or certification programs? These can provide substantial income while furthering your mission.

Then there's the power of individual donors. People love to support causes they feel personally connected to. Cultivating relationships with individual donors can not only provide a steady income stream but also build a community of advocates for your cause. It's important to remember that small, regular donations can add up to make a big impact over time.

Another avenue is social enterprise. Nonprofits can create business ventures that align with their mission, generating income while making a social impact. Whether it's selling eco-friendly products or providing job training in a cafe setting, social enterprises can become a significant and sustainable source of revenue.

Corporate partnerships can also go beyond traditional philanthropy. Many businesses seek to fulfill their corporate social responsibility goals and may be open to innovative partnerships that provide value to both sides. This could range from cause marketing campaigns to shared value initiatives where both the nonprofit and the corporation can benefit.

Membership programs are another way to generate funds. By offering memberships, you offer stakeholders a way to be more deeply involved with your organization. In return for their annual or monthly contributions, members can receive benefits like exclusive updates, event invitations, or special access to your services.

Crowdfunding and online fundraising campaigns can also harness the power of your supporters, especially for specific projects or initiatives. These campaigns not only raise funds but also increase your visibility and can attract new donors.

Lastly, don't forget about in-kind contributions. Sometimes support doesn't come in the form of money. Donations of goods, services, or expertise can reduce expenses and free up other resources for direct mission-related work.

The pursuit of financial sustainability for a nonprofit is akin to assembling a jigsaw puzzle. Grants are just one piece. A robust financial strategy incorporates multiple sources of income, blending traditional and innovative approaches. By diversifying your revenue streams, you not only secure your organization's future but also give yourself the flexibility to adapt and grow in response to changing circumstances.

Chapter 14
Do More with the Right Less

In the nonprofit world, there's a pervasive myth that doing more—more programs, more services, more activities—automatically equates to greater impact. But the truth is, effectiveness doesn't come from volume; it comes from focus. Doing more with less isn't about cutting corners or scaling back mission-critical work. It's about honing in on what you do best and executing it with precision. It's about doing more with the right less.

Take a hard look at your programs and initiatives. Ask yourself: Which of these are truly aligned with our core mission? Which ones are making the most significant impact? It's not about being busy; it's about being impactful. When you strip away the non-essential, what you have left is the potent core of your work—the programs that deliver the most value to your community.

This approach requires rigorous evaluation and sometimes tough decisions. It may mean sunsetting programs that are dear to your heart but are no longer serving your mission as powerfully as others. It requires clarity and courage to say no to good opportunities so that you can say yes to great ones.

Doing more with the right less also means leveraging your resources wisely. It's about using technology not just for the sake of modernization, but to genuinely enhance productivity and outreach. It's about deploying your team's talents where they can shine brightest and have the most significant effect.

Moreover, this philosophy extends to your fundraising efforts. Rather than casting a wide and generic net, focus on targeted campaigns that resonate deeply with the specific segments of donors who are most aligned with your work. A personalized approach can yield better results than mass appeals.

It's also about fostering partnerships and collaborations that multiply impact. Instead of trying to do everything in-house, look for opportunities to work with others. When nonprofits combine forces, share resources, and align efforts, they can tackle challenges more efficiently and effectively.

Remember, doing more with the right less is not about scarcity; it's about selectivity and smart growth. It's about making every effort count, every dollar stretch further, and every program shine brighter. It's not minimizing your goals; it's maximizing your resources.

In a culture that often equates busy with successful, it's revolutionary to focus on less—but not just any less. The right less. This is how you magnify your impact, deepen your reach, and advance your mission with intention and integrity.

Chapter 15
Build Movements, Not Organizations

Many nonprofit leaders fixate on the organization itself—its size, its reputation, its financial growth. But the most successful nonprofits understand that the real power lies not within the walls of an organization, but within the hearts of the people they engage. These nonprofits aren't just building organizations; they're igniting movements.

A movement transcends your organization. It's a cause that people can rally behind, a collective effort that empowers individuals to become part of something larger than themselves. When you build a movement, you're not just seeking donors or volunteers; you're cultivating activists and advocates for your cause.

So how do you spark a movement? First, it's about articulating a clear and compelling vision—one that speaks to the values and aspirations of a broad community, not just your immediate stakeholders. This vision should be bold, it should be inclusive, and it should call people to action.

Communicating your message in a way that resonates is key. Movements are built on stories—stories of struggle, stories of change, stories of hope. Your job is to tell these stories in a way that connects emotionally and inspires action. This means being authentic, being consistent, and being ready to amplify the voices of those you serve.

Creating a movement also means decentralizing control. Rather than holding tightly to your programs and brand, you give your supporters the tools and freedom to make the cause their own. You might provide them with resources to host events, raise funds, or spread awareness in their own way. When people feel ownership over a piece of the movement, their commitment deepens.

Moreover, movements thrive on collaboration. They break down silos between organizations and foster partnerships across sectors. They recognize that no one organization has all the answers or resources, and that by working together, we can achieve much more than any of us could achieve alone.

Lastly, movements measure success differently. It's not just about the number of dollars raised or the number of programs delivered; it's about the scale of change created. It's about shifts in public perception, changes in policy, and the empowerment of communities. These are the metrics that matter in a movement.

Remember, an organization can close its doors, but a movement continues to ripple through society. By focusing on building a movement, you ensure that your mission endures beyond the lifespan of any single entity. You create a legacy of change that can carry forward for generations to come.

Chapter 16
Sustainable Impact over Quick Exits

In a world that glorifies the quick win and the dramatic exit, nonprofits stand as beacons of a different kind of value—sustainable impact. The path to profound social change is rarely a sprint; it's a marathon. It's not about launching a flashy initiative only to move on to the next thing; it's about commitment, about digging in for the long haul to ensure that the change you create lasts.

Sustainable impact requires patience and perseverance. It means setting up systems and structures that ensure your work continues, regardless of funding cycles or shifts in leadership. It's about building a foundation strong enough to support not just the current generation but those to come.

This long-term thinking also influences how you measure success. Instead of short-term metrics, focus on indicators that reflect lasting change. Look beyond immediate outputs and consider the outcomes and long-term effects of your work. How are you transforming lives? How are you altering systems? These are the measures of sustainable impact.

Creating sustainable impact also means investing in the community you serve. It's not enough to provide services; you must empower the community to lead and sustain those services. This might involve training local leaders, supporting grassroots initiatives, or advocating for policy changes that will continue to bear fruit long after your direct involvement ends.

Financial sustainability is another critical aspect. This means diversifying your funding sources and developing revenue streams that aren't solely reliant on grants or donations. Think about social enterprises, partnerships, and other innovative models that can provide ongoing support for your mission.

Moreover, sustainable impact comes from a willingness to adapt. What works today may not work tomorrow. Nonprofits committed to lasting change must be nimble, able to pivot and evolve in response to new challenges and opportunities. This agility ensures that your organization remains relevant and effective over time.

Finally, sustainable impact is about legacy. It's about what you leave behind. As a nonprofit leader, your greatest achievement might not be a project you complete but the capacity you build within your organization and community. It's the systems you establish, the knowledge you disseminate, and the empowerment you facilitate.

In the end, sustainable impact isn't as flashy as the quick wins that dominate headlines. But the quiet work of building resilience, fostering community, and planting seeds for the future is where the true transformation lies. This is the work that endures. It's the difference between making a splash and making a difference.

Chapter 17
Stay Agile and Adaptable

In the dynamic landscape of social change, adaptability isn't just a buzzword—it's a survival skill. For nonprofits, the ability to pivot in response to shifting needs, emerging trends, and unexpected challenges is what keeps an organization relevant and effective. Agility is your greatest asset in a world where change is the only constant.

Agility means staying light on your feet, ready to take on new opportunities or to step back and reassess when something isn't working. It's recognizing that even the best-laid plans might need to be altered when they meet the complex realities on the ground. It's understanding that what worked yesterday may not work tomorrow, and being willing to evolve without losing sight of your core mission.

To be agile, your nonprofit must cultivate a culture that encourages innovation, where new ideas are welcomed and tested. It's a place where failure isn't feared but seen as a valuable learning experience. Create an environment where your team feels safe to experiment, to question the status quo, and to take calculated risks.

Adaptability also means keeping a close ear to the ground. Listen to the communities you serve; they are the best indicators of what's needed and what's working. Foster strong relationships that allow for honest feedback and open dialogue. This direct line to those you're aiming to help will guide you in making real-time adjustments that increase your impact.

Stay informed about the wider world, too. Changes in technology, policy, and society can all dramatically affect your work. By being aware of these external factors, you can anticipate shifts rather than being blindsided by them.

Financial agility is crucial. Diversify your funding streams to cushion against economic shocks. Embrace technology and new platforms that can make your work more efficient and expand your reach. And always be ready to reallocate resources where they're most needed, even if it means stopping a project that's no longer viable.

Remember, adaptability is not about changing your values or mission; it's about finding new ways to achieve your goals. It's not about compromise; it's about effectiveness. It's not about following every new trend; it's about discerning which changes are meaningful and will enhance your work.

Nonprofits that thrive are those that blend steadfast commitment with the flexibility to navigate a changing world. They know that to stay true to their cause, they must be willing to evolve how they pursue it. In essence, to stay agile and adaptable is to ensure that your nonprofit not only survives but flourishes, making the greatest possible impact for those you serve.

Part 3
Making Moves

Chapter 18
Constraints Foster Creativity

Conventional wisdom might lead you to believe that the more resources you have, the greater your nonprofit's impact can be. However, the truth is often counterintuitive: constraints are not your enemy; they are your muse. Limitations can spur innovation and force you to think creatively, pushing your organization to new heights.

When you face limitations, whether in budget, time, or manpower, you're pushed to look at problems from different angles. Constraints challenge you to question every assumption, to do more with less, and to cut through what's non-essential. This is where creativity thrives—innovative solutions often emerge from the pressure of having fewer options.

In the nonprofit realm, resources are almost always tight. This scarcity is not a hurdle to lament over; it's an opportunity to explore. It can lead to more effective programs that are designed to maximize impact per dollar spent, rather than sprawling projects that consume funds without delivering proportional results.

Encourage your team to embrace constraints as a challenge. Make it a game: What's the most impactful initiative we can launch with the resources at hand? How can we increase our outreach with the current staff? Such questions drive ingenuity, leading to grassroots campaigns that cost little but resonate deeply or to volunteer-driven projects that achieve what money alone could not.

Remember, creativity isn't about abundance; it's about making remarkable things happen within the boundaries you operate in. It's about turning constraints into advantages. Think of the most successful campaigns or programs that have come out of the nonprofit sector—they often started as a simple, constrained idea that was executed brilliantly.

Moreover, constraints force you to focus. They compel you to be disciplined with your resources and to prioritize what truly matters. This focus can lead to a stronger brand, clearer messaging, and more strategic decision-making.

Don't wait for the perfect moment when all resources are available—that time rarely comes. Instead, act now, within the constraints you face, and let those limitations guide you to creative, innovative, and resourceful solutions. Through this, your nonprofit can prove that creativity doesn't require deep pockets, just deep commitment to making every resource count.

Remember, it's not about the size of your budget; it's the size of your ideas and the depth of your passion that truly make a difference. Embrace your constraints, and watch as they become the catalyst for your nonprofit's most creative solutions.

Chapter 19
Quality Over Quantity in Service

In the nonprofit sector, the temptation to measure success by the number of people served or programs delivered is common. But numbers alone can mislead. True impact is not always about reaching more people; it's about making a profound difference in the lives you touch. Quality over quantity in service is not just a mantra; it's a strategic approach that can lead to deeper, more sustainable change.

When you focus on the quality of your service, you invest in the individual stories, the one-on-one moments that don't make for grand statistics but create real transformation. A single well-run program that genuinely improves the quality of life for a handful can be more valuable than a dozen hastily organized initiatives that only scratch the surface of need.

Emphasizing quality means listening intently to the communities you serve. It involves understanding the complex web of challenges they face and responding with services that are not just a temporary fix but a step towards lasting betterment. Tailored programs that consider the unique context of your beneficiaries can achieve outcomes that quantity-focused efforts often overlook.

Quality service requires a commitment to evaluation and continuous improvement. It means setting high standards for your work and being diligent in meeting them. This often involves gathering detailed feedback, learning from it, and refining your approach. The question always at hand is, "How can we make our services more effective and meaningful?"

In the world of nonprofits, your reputation is your currency. By concentrating on quality, you build a reputation for excellence and trustworthiness. This, in turn, attracts more supporters, volunteers, and donors who are inspired by your high-impact work.

Moreover, a quality-focused approach can lead to more sustainable programs. When you solve problems effectively, even at a smaller scale, you set the stage for your initiatives to be models for replication. This can amplify your impact far beyond the initial scope of work.

It's also about recognizing that each person you help is a world unto themselves, and when you change one life profoundly, the ripple effect can be enormous. It can inspire a community, influence policy, and even redefine what's possible in your field.

Strive for the kind of quality in your service that becomes the hallmark of your nonprofit. Let each program you run, each person you help, each story you change be a testament to the power of profound, rather than prolific, service.

Let's redefine success in the nonprofit sector not by the quantity of services delivered but by the quality of change achieved. Let's make every effort count, profoundly.

Chapter 20
Focus on the Core Mission

Every nonprofit begins with a spark—a core mission that ignites action. It's the fundamental reason for your existence, the guiding light for every decision and initiative. Yet, in the hustle of fundraising, program development, and daily operations, that core mission can get clouded by distractions and side ventures. Staying laser-focused on your core mission is crucial, not just for clarity of purpose but also for the potency of your impact.

Focusing on your core mission means saying no to projects that don't align, no matter how tempting they may be. It's about recognizing that every resource spent on a divergent path is a resource not spent on your main goal. When you dilute your efforts, you dilute your effectiveness. It's not just about doing good; it's about doing the right good.

Remember, your core mission is your brand. It's what people think of when they hear your nonprofit's name. It's what draws in donors, volunteers, and advocates. When you stay true to your mission, you build a stronger, more cohesive brand identity. This focus creates a narrative that resonates with your audience, compelling them to join and support your cause with conviction.

Staying mission-focused also simplifies decision-making. Each opportunity or challenge can be approached with a simple question: Does this advance our core mission? If the answer is no, you have a clear justification to pass and move on. This approach keeps your strategy clean and your path forward clear.

But how do you maintain this focus? It starts with your leadership—ensuring that every team member understands and is committed to the mission. It extends to your operations—structuring programs and initiatives that are direct expressions of your core purpose. And it permeates your communications—crafting messages that consistently highlight the mission and its importance.

Moreover, a mission-focused nonprofit attracts and retains talent that is passionate about the cause. When team members are aligned with the mission, they bring not just their skills but also their hearts to the work, leading to a more motivated, dedicated, and impactful organization.

Finally, focusing on your core mission ensures that you make a deep, rather than wide, impact. You become specialists, experts in your field, capable of driving significant change in your area of focus. This depth of expertise makes you a go-to resource, elevates your credibility, and ultimately amplifies your impact.

In conclusion, let your core mission be the unwavering star by which you navigate the waters of nonprofit work. When you focus on what you set out to do, you build a more impactful, respected, and sustainable organization.

Chapter 21
Big Visions Start with Small Details

Dream big. It's the mantra of every visionary. But while dreaming, don't trip over the details. Nonprofits start with monumental visions — ending hunger, curing diseases, transforming education. But these aren't achieved in one fell swoop. They're built like a mosaic: one tiny, carefully placed piece at a time.

In the nonprofit world, sweating the small stuff isn't just recommended; it's required. Your big, hairy, audacious goal won't stand up if it's not on a foundation of gritty particulars. That database of donors, the timing of your newsletters, the precision in your grant writing — these are the pixels in your picture.

Picture this: a fundraising campaign that's set to launch without a hitch. But someone forgot to test the donation page under heavy load. It crashes. The grand vision of a world-changing influx of donations is lost to a technicality. The devil isn't just in the details. Sometimes, it is the detail.

You might not think that proofreading that email for the tenth time matters. It does. To someone, it's the difference between hitting donate and delete. The extra volunteer training session you squeezed into the schedule? That's the difference between a good event and a transformative one.

It's easy to get lost in strategy sessions, dreaming of what your nonprofit will do a year from now, five years from now. But what about today? What small step can you take right now that will inch you closer to that vision? These steps are unglamorous. They're the proofreading, the thank-you calls, the inventory checks at the end of a long day. Yet they matter immensely.

You want to change the world. Don't just build a mission statement. Build a detail-oriented culture. Get the small things right, and the big things have a way of falling into place. But if you ignore the details in favor of the dream, you may find the vision is just that — a dream.

People praise nonprofits for their big wins. The campaigns that change public policy, the movements that mobilize millions. But ask any nonprofit leader who's actually moved the needle, and they'll tell you about the groundwork. They'll tell you that changing the world starts with changing a font so it's readable, with coding a website so it's navigable, with scheduling social media posts so they're seen.

Every time you obsess over a detail, you're putting another penny in the piggy bank of your grand vision. And believe it or not, those pennies add up. They add up to trust, to credibility, to the next donation, and the one after that. Until one day, you step back, and you see not just a collection of details, but a masterpiece of impact.

Big visions need broad strokes, but they're nothing without the fine ones. So, go ahead and dream. But never forget that the magic is in the minutiae.

Chapter 22
Decisive Action Moves Missions Forward

When you're working for a cause, there's an unspoken rule that seems to permeate the atmosphere: 'Be careful. Don't rush. Weigh every option.' But here's a truth that sparks change: Missions thrive on decisiveness, not on hesitation.

In the nonprofit realm, the weight of responsibility can be paralyzing. Every decision seems to carry the burden of a hundred outcomes, each one tied to a person, a place, an ideal. But the moments that lead to milestones are often the ones seized quickly. Why? Because decisiveness is a catalyst. It propels you forward, and movement—any movement—is better than a standstill.

Consider this: every minute spent deliberating over the pros and cons of a potentially beneficial program is a minute not spent making an impact. Yes, reckless abandon is not the answer, but neither is over-caution. The middle ground is where you find the sweet spot—quick, informed decisions made with the mission in mind.

Decisiveness does not equate to impulsiveness. It's not about choosing speed over quality. It's about understanding that perfect conditions are a myth. Waiting for the ideal set of circumstances is like waiting for a train that's never going to arrive. And while you wait, opportunities pass by—unnoticed and unseized.

This is not an argument against planning or foresight. It's a call to action when the path aligns with your goals—even if you can't see the end of the road. Bold moves unsettle the status quo, and for a nonprofit looking to cut through the noise, to make a mark, unsettling is necessary.

Remember, actions echo louder in the halls of progress than the most eloquent plans. Plans are static; actions ripple. They create waves, and waves create change. Every big mission in history started with a single act—a decision to move.

So, when the next opportunity arises, an event to partner with, a grant to apply for, a program that could amplify your reach—pause, assess quickly, and if it fits—act. There will always be a million 'what ifs' but focus instead on the 'what can be.'

The world needs more than cautious contemplation; it needs your mission in motion. Be decisive, and let that decisiveness be the engine of your impact. After all, missions are not just planned; they are executed—one decisive step at a time.

Chapter 23
Curate Your Initiatives

Imagine your nonprofit's projects are like a museum's art collection. Each initiative, like each piece of art, tells a part of your story, contributes to your mission, and reflects your values. But a museum doesn't display every piece it owns at once. It curates the collection, carefully selecting what to show to make the biggest impact. Your nonprofit should curate its initiatives in the same way.

Curating isn't about limiting your vision but clarifying it. It's about focusing on what you do best and what aligns most closely with your mission. In the nonprofit sector, the temptation is to be all things to all people. There's so much need, so many good causes, that it's hard to say no. But when you spread yourself too thin, you dilute your impact.

When you curate your initiatives, you make tough choices. You prioritize. You may even stop doing things that are good but not great or aligned but not essential. This isn't about stepping back; it's about stepping up the quality and coherence of what you do.

This process begins with a deep understanding of your strengths and your community's needs. What can your organization do better than anyone else? What unique value do you bring to the table? Use these answers as your criteria for selection. When an opportunity arises, ask not just if you can do it, but if you should. Does it fit within the "exhibit" you're trying to create?

Curating also means being strategic with your resources. It's recognizing that not every "good" opportunity is a "right" opportunity for you. It's acknowledging that saying "yes" to everything actually means you're not saying "yes" to anything with full commitment. Instead, invest your time, talent, and funds into initiatives that truly showcase the best of what your nonprofit stands for.

Remember, curation is an active, ongoing process. It's not enough to do it once and then rest on your laurels. Regularly review your initiatives. Are they still relevant? Are they making an impact? Are they reflecting your nonprofit's mission? This process ensures that you remain focused and that your impact grows stronger, not just wider.

In curating your initiatives, you also build a stronger narrative for your stakeholders. Donors, volunteers, and the communities you serve can clearly see what you stand for and the difference you're making. They can walk through the "gallery" of your work and understand the story you're telling. And like any great exhibit, they'll be inspired, engaged, and moved to support your cause.

In conclusion, curating your initiatives is about quality over quantity. It's about making the most impact with what you have by carefully selecting where to focus your energies. By curating your initiatives, your nonprofit becomes not just a collection of projects, but a coherent, impactful exhibition of your mission in action.

Chapter 24
Less Noise, More Signal

In the digital age, everyone's vying for attention. Tweets, updates, newsletters, and alerts—it's a constant battle against the noise. For nonprofits, the challenge is not just to get noticed but to make sure what's noticed matters. It's about ensuring the signal outweighs the noise.

Your signal is your mission's voice, the clear, resonant message that cuts through the cacophony. It's not just about being louder; it's about being truer. In a world where everyone is shouting, the temptation is to shout louder. But what's needed is not more volume, but more clarity.

Less noise means more focus. Every tweet, every email, every update should serve a purpose. Does this message advance your cause? Does it inform, inspire, or call to action? If the answer is no, it's just noise. Remember, when you communicate without a clear purpose, you're not just filling someone's inbox or feed—you're depleting your own currency of attention.

More signal means more substance. It's about quality over quantity. One well-crafted, meaningful message can do more for your mission than a hundred forgettable posts. Think of your communications as a beacon, not a broadcast. You want to guide your audience to your cause, not just announce your existence.

In practice, creating more signal means being strategic with your communications. It means being deliberate about what you share and when. It's about crafting messages that resonate with your core audience and reflect the depth of your commitment to your mission. This might mean communicating less often, but with greater impact.

It also means listening. A strong signal is not just about output; it's about interaction. Engage with your audience, respond to their concerns, and build a community around your cause. When your audience feels heard, they pay closer attention to what you say.

In essence, less noise and more signal is about respect. Respect for your mission, respect for your audience's time, and respect for the importance of your message. It's about cutting through the clutter with messages that are thoughtful, meaningful, and impactful.

In conclusion, as you craft your nonprofit's message, remember that your goal is not to add to the noise but to amplify the signal. In doing so, you honor your mission, engage your community, and make a lasting impression that echoes beyond the immediate clamor. That's how you turn communication into connection and noise into action.

Chapter 25
Embrace Enduring Values

Values are the compass that guides a nonprofit organization. They're the enduring beliefs that anchor us in turbulent times and the stars we navigate by when charting our course through the sea of societal challenges. Embracing enduring values isn't a statement of what we aspire to be someday; it's a declaration of who we are today, every day.

For nonprofits, values are not a marketing strategy or a decorative plaque on the wall. They are lived experiences, the DNA of the organization. They inform every decision, interaction, and goal. When values are clear, they permeate the fabric of the nonprofit, becoming evident in every program, campaign, and conversation.

Enduring values are timeless. They don't fluctuate with trends or bend under pressure. They are the bedrock upon which missions are built and legacies are left. Whether it's integrity, compassion, equity, or innovation, these values are the pillars that uphold your efforts and the legacy you strive to create.

To truly embrace these values, a nonprofit must embody them authentically and consistently. This means going beyond mere words; it means operationalizing values so they're evident in how you treat your employees, design your programs, and engage with your community. It's about making hard choices that align with these values even when it's inconvenient or unpopular.

In embracing enduring values, there's a potent force of differentiation for your organization. In a world brimming with causes and initiatives, it's your values that can set you apart. People are drawn to authenticity and can discern the genuine from the superficial. When your values are deeply ingrained, they attract those who share them, forging stronger, more meaningful connections.

Moreover, in times of crisis or difficult decision-making, these values become your guideposts. They help you navigate complex situations with a sense of purpose and direction. When others might be swayed by the winds of circumstance, your nonprofit can stand firm, knowing its course is true.

Living out your values also invites accountability. It means being open to scrutiny, welcoming dialogue about your practices, and being willing to make changes when there's misalignment. It's a continuous process of reflection and action that keeps your organization aligned with its core principles.

In conclusion, embrace enduring values not as slogans but as standards to live by. They are the soul of your nonprofit, the essence that brings life to your mission. When you embrace and embody these values, you build an organization that's not just effective but also respected and revered. You create a legacy that transcends the moment and touches the future.

Chapter 26
The Integrity of Your Mission

At the heart of every nonprofit lies its mission – the central purpose that gives meaning to its efforts and defines its existence. The integrity of your mission is the commitment to stay true to this purpose in every action and decision. It's a steadfast adherence that communicates to the world, "This is who we are; this is what we stand for."

A mission with integrity is non-negotiable; it's not for sale, and it doesn't bend to fit the convenience of the moment or the lure of easy funding. It's a beacon that shines consistently, whether in the spotlight of public acclaim or the quiet of a routine day. It guides your strategies, your programs, and even the partnerships you cultivate.

Maintaining the integrity of your mission means you evaluate every opportunity not just on its potential benefits, but on its alignment with your purpose. Will this new initiative advance your cause? Does this potential partnership share your fundamental values? If the answer veers towards no, the path forward is clear – no matter how attractive the opportunity might seem.

In practice, the integrity of your mission manifests in transparent operations and honest communications. It's about showing the impact of donations and grants in clear, tangible ways. It's about being upfront about successes and failures alike. When the public trusts that your nonprofit is mission-driven, their support solidifies, and their advocacy amplifies.

But maintaining this integrity isn't just about external perceptions; it's also about internal consistency. It's ensuring that the mission is not just a concept for the leadership team but a lived experience for every employee and volunteer. When staff members at all levels understand and connect with the mission, their work becomes more than a job; it becomes a part of a larger story of change and impact.

This deep connection to the mission can also inspire innovation. When you're committed to a purpose, you look for creative ways to advance it. You're willing to explore uncharted paths and embrace new ideas that can bring your mission to life in powerful, impactful ways.

However, the integrity of your mission is tested in times of challenge. Economic downturns, shifts in political landscapes, and social upheavals can all pressure a nonprofit to stray from its path. It's during these times that your unwavering commitment becomes most crucial. It's also when it becomes most visible, as stakeholders watch to see if the mission is truly at the core of all you do.

In conclusion, the integrity of your mission is your anchor and your greatest strength. It attracts the right supporters, drives impactful work, and sustains the organization through both triumphs and trials. Preserve it, protect it, and let it be the measure of your success. For a nonprofit, the integrity of the mission isn't just a part of the strategy; it is the strategy.

Chapter 27
Repurpose to Amplify Your Impact

In the lifecycle of a nonprofit, resources – whether time, materials, or funds – are often scarce. This scarcity need not be a constraint but a catalyst for innovation. By learning to repurpose what you already have, you can amplify your impact without stretching your resources thin.

Repurposing is an art form within the nonprofit sector. It's about looking at the tools, programs, and materials at your disposal through a lens of creativity and adaptability. A community center's old library can become a hub for after-school tutoring. Excess supplies from a health campaign could be turned into educational kits for schools. The possibilities are only as limited as your imagination.

But repurposing goes beyond physical resources. It's also about reallocating your organization's time and talent where they can be most effective. Perhaps the skills developed in one program can be transferred to another. Or maybe the insights from a completed project can inform a new initiative, streamlining the planning process and increasing the probability of success.

This mindset also encourages sustainability. By repurposing materials, you reduce waste and promote a model of operation that aligns with the values of environmental stewardship – a growing concern for donors, volunteers, and the communities you serve. It's a powerful statement: your nonprofit doesn't just deliver impact; it does so while being mindful of its ecological footprint.

Moreover, repurposing aligns with the fundamental nonprofit ethos of doing more with less. It's about maximizing impact while maintaining lean operations. It's a rejection of the notion that effectiveness is directly proportional to the amount spent. Instead, it's an embrace of the idea that effectiveness is about the smart utilization and redistribution of available resources.

When you repurpose effectively, you also tell a story of resourcefulness and resilience. This narrative is compelling to supporters and can open doors to new partnerships. It shows that your organization is innovative and determined, capable of navigating the complex challenges of nonprofit work.

Internally, this approach can foster a culture of creativity and empowerment. When staff and volunteers are encouraged to think about repurposing, they engage more deeply with their work. They see themselves as active agents of change, capable of generating new life from existing resources.

In your communication with the public and donors, highlight these repurposing successes. Share how an old program was reimagined to meet a new need, or how surplus from one project became the seed for another. These stories illustrate your nonprofit's commitment to impactful and efficient work.

In summary, repurposing is not just about using old things in new ways; it's a strategic approach that speaks to the adaptability and sustainability of your nonprofit. It amplifies your impact by making the most of every resource, engages your community with a narrative of innovation, and demonstrates a commitment to sustainable practice. Embrace repurposing, and watch your impact grow.

Chapter 28
It's a Marathon, Not a Sprint

In the world of nonprofits, urgency is a common sentiment. There's always a pressing need, a group that requires immediate assistance, a problem that demands instant attention. But here's the truth: real, sustainable change is a marathon, not a sprint. It's not about the speed at which you address the issue but the persistence, endurance, and consistency of your efforts over time. When you treat your mission as a sprint, you run the risk of burnout—both for your staff and your organization. You chase funding, leap at every opportunity, and stretch your resources thin, all in the name of immediate impact. But lasting change—the kind that truly transforms lives and systems—is built step by step, over long periods.

This long-term perspective reshapes how you approach every aspect of your work. Instead of short-term campaigns that spike in intensity and then fizzle out, you invest in long-term strategies that gradually build momentum. You nurture relationships with donors instead of just soliciting one-time gifts. You develop programs that are sustainable and scalable, not just flash-in-the-pan successes.

The marathon mindset also changes how you measure success. Rather than only celebrating big, immediate wins, you value steady progress. You recognize that small steps forward are still movement in the right direction. And when you look back over months and years, these small steps compound into significant strides toward your mission.

Adopting a marathon approach doesn't mean you ignore the acute needs in front of you; it means you address them with an eye on the horizon. You're not just putting out fires; you're also building a more fire-resistant future. You're planting seeds that will grow over time, not just harvesting what's already grown.

Moreover, pacing yourself allows for reflection and adaptation. When you're sprinting, you're reacting. When you're running a marathon, you're strategizing, adjusting your pace, and conserving energy for the hills ahead. You can pivot as the landscape changes, ensuring your nonprofit remains relevant and effective.

In the marathon of nonprofit work, it's also important to pass the baton. Succession planning ensures that when one leader tires, another is ready to take over, keeping the pace without losing ground. Building a team that shares the load, with diverse skills and the same dedication to the cause, ensures that the organization can sustain its momentum, even as individual players change.

In conclusion, treating your nonprofit mission as a marathon means embracing the long game. It's about endurance, resilience, and a steady pace towards a more impactful finish line. When you commit to the marathon, you're not just running; you're going the distance, making sure the change you create is as enduring as your commitment to the cause.

Part 4
Competition

Chapter 29
Collaboration Over Competition

In the universe of nonprofit work, the adage 'two heads are better than one' holds an especially poignant truth. The challenges faced are too vast for any one entity to tackle alone. Collaboration isn't just a nice-to-have; it's a must-have. It's the lever that can amplify impact and accelerate change.

The traditional market mindset pitches organizations against each other, battling for market share. In the nonprofit sector, the 'market' is impact, and the 'share' is social good. Here, competition becomes counterproductive. If the goal is to maximize benefit, then collaboration trumps competition every time.

Collaborating with other nonprofits, community groups, businesses, and governments can lead to shared resources, knowledge, and manpower, all directed towards common goals. It means pooling expertise to solve complex problems more effectively than going it alone. In this realm, success is not zero-sum. One organization's gain in efficacy or reach is a win for the collective cause.

For example, consider the global push for clean water. A single organization might fund wells in a community, another might specialize in sanitation education, and a third might advocate for policy changes. Working in silos, they make ripples; together, they create waves. The well-funded organization's structures are better maintained thanks to the education provided by the second, and the third's advocacy ensures sustainable practices are supported by law. This is the multiplier effect of collaborative effort.

However, for collaboration to be more than just a buzzword, it requires a framework. It needs open communication, shared objectives, and mutual respect. This might mean regular roundtables with local nonprofits or joining forces on larger initiatives. It also calls for humility – recognizing that you don't have all the answers and that others bring valuable insights to the table.

Collaboration extends to how nonprofits engage with their communities. The voices of those you're aiming to help should be at the forefront of what you do. Involving community members in the decision-making process ensures that efforts are relevant and responsive to their needs. This participatory approach is the epitome of meaningful collaboration.

Additionally, when nonprofits collaborate, they send a powerful message to funders. They demonstrate a commitment to efficiency and impact, rather than territorialism and brand ego. This can be compelling to donors who want to see their contributions go further.

Moreover, collaboration doesn't mean losing identity; it means strengthening it by being part of a larger narrative of change. It allows nonprofits to specialize and excel in their niche, confident that allies are covering other bases. Like threads in a tapestry, each organization's unique contribution is vital to the integrity and beauty of the whole.

The pivot from competition to collaboration is both a mindset and a strategy. It's about seeing beyond the boundaries of your nonprofit to the bigger picture of social good. It's about recognizing that, in the pursuit of change, the combined strength of many is greater than the isolated efforts of one.

Embrace collaboration, and watch as the barriers to change become surmountable, not through rivalry, but through the power of unity and shared purpose.

Chapter 30
Embrace Your Community's Growth

For nonprofits, the true metric of success is measured not in dollars raised or the number of programs delivered, but in the palpable growth of the community they serve. Growth in the nonprofit context isn't just about scaling up; it's about deepening roots and expanding the capacity for community self-sustenance and resilience.

Embracing your community's growth means understanding that the health of your nonprofit is inextricably linked to the health of the community. It's recognizing that every community has a unique set of strengths, challenges, and aspirations, and that sustainable growth caters to these nuances rather than imposing one-size-fits-all solutions.

But what does community growth look like? It can be seen in the increased confidence of individuals to lead projects, in the collaborative spirit that solves neighborhood issues, or in the strengthened network of support for the most vulnerable. It's also reflected in the youth who are inspired to take initiative because they have seen the positive impact close to home.

Invest in the people. Equip them with skills, knowledge, and opportunities to improve their circumstances. When community members grow in capability, the entire community rises. Initiatives that might include leadership training programs, educational workshops, and mentorship opportunities all contribute to a foundation of community empowerment.

Celebrate the small wins as much as the large. The community garden that thrives, the local volunteer day with record turnout, or the success of a community-led fundraiser are all indications of a community coming into its own. These wins create a narrative of positive change that fuels further growth.

Stay responsive to the community's changing needs. As the community grows, its needs will evolve. What was a priority one year might be replaced by a new challenge or opportunity the next. Nonprofits must remain agile, adapting to these shifts with the community's input as their guide.

Furthermore, fostering community growth often means stepping back to let local leaders emerge. This might seem counterintuitive in the hustle of nonprofit activity, but space must be given for new voices to be heard and for community-driven initiatives to take the lead. Your role evolves from initiator to supporter, from leading to partnering.

In this journey, remember to document and share the stories of growth. These narratives are potent—they inspire, attract support, and reinforce the value of the work being done. They show the community's trajectory of growth, turning abstract numbers into real-world evidence of progress.

Also, be open to the organic, sometimes unpredictable, ways in which communities grow. This might mean supporting a grassroots project that doesn't neatly fit into your predefined strategy but has the potential for significant impact. It's about being flexible enough to recognize and nurture the seeds of community-led innovation.

In sum, embracing your community's growth is a commitment to a shared journey. It's understanding that a nonprofit's success is not just in leading change but in nurturing an environment where the community can sustain and expand that change from within. It's about moving beyond the role of provider to that of partner, celebrating every step forward, and recognizing that each stride benefits all.

Chapter 31
Prioritize with Your Mission

In the whirlwind of running a nonprofit, you're bombarded with decisions daily. With each new challenge and opportunity, you'll find a crossroad: do I adhere to the mission or take a shortcut? The guiding star for these decisions, the uncompromising principle, should always be your mission.

Prioritizing with your mission means making it the lens through which all decisions are made. It's not just a statement to be framed on the wall or added to the footer of your website; it's the DNA of your organization, the core from which everything else unfolds.

To do this effectively, you must ensure that everyone in the organization, from the board to the volunteers, understands and embraces the mission. It should resonate with them on a personal level. When the mission is clear, it simplifies decisions. Does this new program align with our mission? Will this partnership advance our cause? If the answer strays from the mission, then you have your answer.

Yet, prioritizing with your mission is not about being inflexible. It's about being focused. It's recognizing that not every good idea is a good idea for you. Your mission serves as a boundary that keeps you from diluting your efforts and ensures that your resources are channeled for the greatest impact.

In practical terms, when you're faced with funding opportunities, evaluate them against the mission. It's tempting to chase funds that seem easily accessible, but if they require you to veer off your path, they're a costly distraction. Remember, when you stay true to your mission, you attract the right kind of support – the kind that doesn't just fund but fuels your cause.

Also, prioritizing with your mission means sometimes saying no to immediate gains for the sake of long-term impact. It's easy to get caught up in the numbers game, measuring success by the volume of services provided or the headcount at events. But if these numbers don't translate into real, mission-driven change, then they're vanity metrics.

Engage your community in this prioritization process as well. Often, they are the ones who feel the impact of your work the most. Their feedback can be invaluable in determining whether an initiative truly serves the mission. Moreover, this inclusive approach strengthens their commitment to your cause, knowing that the mission is not just a statement but a lived experience.

Periodic reviews of how your activities align with the mission can keep your nonprofit on course. This is not just about auditing finances but evaluating whether each aspect of your work still serves the core purpose. It's an opportunity to reaffirm or recalibrate, ensuring that your trajectory aligns with your mission.

In conclusion, prioritize with your mission, and let it be the constant in the variable world of nonprofit work. It's the filter for opportunities, the measure of success, and the voice that says "this is who we are." When you are steadfast in your mission, you not only preserve the integrity of your organization but also amplify its power to make a difference.

Chapter 32
Ground-level Excellence

Excellence in the nonprofit sector is not a banner to be waved from the distant heights of boardrooms or the detached strategies of high-level meetings. It is a commitment to quality that begins at the ground level, with the hands and hearts that touch the lives you aim to change.

Ground-level excellence means delivering services with a level of care and attention that speaks to the dignity of every individual you serve. It's about ensuring that every meal served, every lesson taught, and every support provided is done with the highest standards of quality and respect.

In the trenches of daily nonprofit work, ground-level excellence is reflected in the small acts that often go unnoticed. It's the volunteer who takes an extra moment to listen, the staff member who goes the extra mile to connect a client with a needed resource, or the administrator who maintains meticulous records to ensure sustainability and accountability.

To foster this kind of excellence, empower your team. Provide them with the training and support they need to do their jobs well. Celebrate the successes, not just in terms of outcomes but also in the quality of the effort. Encourage initiative and provide space for creativity; often, those at the ground level know best how to improve the processes they're involved in every day.

This commitment to excellence must be systemic. It's about creating an environment where quality is the norm, not the exception. It means having clear standards, regular feedback loops, and a culture that asks, "How can we do this better?" It's a culture that's not afraid to iterate and learn from both successes and failures.

Ground-level excellence is also about consistency. The

populations served by nonprofits often deal with instability in various forms, and your organization can be a rock of reliability in their shifting sands. Whether it's a community center that opens its doors without fail or a hotline that always has someone ready to answer, dependability is a cornerstone of excellence.

It's crucial that this pursuit of excellence is inclusive. Engaging those you serve in assessing the quality of programs ensures that excellence is not just an internal standard but one that resonates with the community's needs and experiences. Feedback from those on the receiving end of your services is a goldmine of insight into how processes and delivery can be refined and improved.

Moreover, ground-level excellence contributes to the narrative of your nonprofit. In a world where stories resonate louder than statistics, the tales of lives touched by genuine care and exceptional service are your most powerful testimonials. These stories become the threads woven into the fabric of your brand and reputation.

In conclusion, ground-level excellence is the practice of embedding quality into the DNA of your organization's daily operations. It's a commitment to the well-being and respect of each person served, the relentless pursuit of improvement, and the steady consistency that builds trust. By championing excellence from the ground up, you lay the foundations for a nonprofit that not only stands out but stands strong in its mission to make a difference.

Chapter 33
The Paper Trail Can Wait

In the nonprofit world, there is an inevitable dance between action and administration. While the latter is crucial for governance, accountability, and the maintenance of a nonprofit's structure, it should never stifle the former. The heart of a nonprofit is in the work it does, not the paperwork it files. The paper trail can wait; the mission cannot.

The tendency to prioritize documentation, reports, and bureaucracy can often lead to missed opportunities. There is a palpable urgency in most nonprofit missions – whether addressing hunger, providing emergency relief, or advocating for social change. When someone needs help, they can't wait for the conclusion of a protracted approval process or the meticulous filling of forms.

This isn't to say that paperwork isn't important. It's essential for tracking progress, securing funding, and ensuring compliance with laws and regulations. But it's about balance and understanding that in the midst of action, sometimes the paperwork must take a back seat.

Operational agility is key in these moments. Being able to mobilize resources, make decisions, and take action quickly can make all the difference in achieving your mission's outcomes. Frontline workers should be empowered to make on-the-spot decisions when necessary, guided by the organization's principles and the immediate needs of those they serve.

Moreover, excessive paperwork can be a demotivating factor for your team, especially when it seems to overshadow the very reason they joined your organization – to make a difference. By simplifying processes and reducing unnecessary bureaucratic overhead, you free up your team to focus on what truly matters: the mission.

Technology can play a significant role in striking this balance. Automating administrative tasks, using project management tools, and implementing efficient data collection systems can significantly reduce the time spent on paperwork, allowing more time for action.

When the paperwork is due, it should be handled efficiently and with the same spirit of service that guides your mission. Reports, forms, and records are narratives of your impact, tools for improvement, and vehicles for accountability. They should tell the story of your work, not become the work itself.

In moments of crisis or great need, remember that flexibility can be your greatest asset. The worth of your nonprofit is measured not by the thickness of your files, but by the depth of your impact. And while a well-documented operation is a responsible one, a responsive and effective operation is an impactful one.

In summary, while a paper trail is necessary, it should not lead or govern the actions of a nonprofit. It's a support system, not a leash. By ensuring that action remains at the forefront of your priorities, you maintain the essence of your mission – to serve, to act, and to make a real-time difference in the lives of those who count on you.

Part 5
Outreach

Chapter 34
The Power of Being Lesser-Known

In a landscape dotted with giant nonprofits, being the lesser-known organization isn't a disadvantage; it's a differentiator. It's easy to get caught up in the race for recognition, to feel the pressure to expand your brand presence at the cost of what really matters—your cause. But there's inherent power in being the underdog, the grassroots entity, the organization that isn't a household name—yet.

Firstly, being lesser-known affords a level of agility that larger organizations might envy. Without the weight of heavy bureaucracy and the scrutiny that comes with wide recognition, your nonprofit can adapt, pivot, and innovate. You can test new ideas, take calculated risks, and make decisions swiftly, learning and evolving in real time.

Secondly, your story is still being written, which means every donor, volunteer, and community member can feel like an integral part of your journey. This isn't just fundraising; it's friend-raising. The connection is personal, the impact of every dollar is evident, and the successes—no matter how small—are shared.

There's also a unique trust that builds within the communities you serve. Without the cynicism that sometimes accompanies larger entities, your nonprofit can establish deep, genuine relationships. People see your work up close. They know your staff by name. Your mission isn't just a statement on a website; it's a living, breathing effort playing out in their backyards.

In this space, your messaging can be bold and focused. With fewer voices in the room, your message doesn't need to be diluted to appeal to the masses. You can speak directly and passionately to those who share your vision. It's not about mass marketing; it's about meaningful conversations. It's about being true to your cause and letting the authenticity of your work speak volumes.

Lastly, there's a certain charm to discovering the hidden gem. When someone stumbles upon your organization and aligns with your mission, the sense of discovery can foster a deeper commitment. It's as if they've been let in on a secret, and they become eager to spread the word in a way that's organic and heartfelt.

So, embrace the power of being lesser-known. Celebrate the flexibility, the intimacy, the freshness of your mission. Use it to fuel your creativity, to galvanize your core supporters, and to carve out a space that's distinctly yours. As you grow—and you will grow—keep the spirit of your early days alive. Because being lesser-known isn't about the size of your impact; it's about the resonance of your message and the passion of your people.

Remember, every giant starts as an underdog. Every widespread movement begins with a whisper. There's power there—embrace it, harness it, and let it propel you forward, one impactful stride at a time.

Chapter 35
Cultivate Your Community

Community isn't just a buzzword. It's the lifeblood of any nonprofit organization. To cultivate a community is to grow your efforts from the ground up, nurturing each relationship and interaction as you would a garden. The fruits of this labor are the lasting bonds that propel your mission forward and the shared commitment that blossoms into change.

At its core, cultivating your community means understanding that your nonprofit exists not above or apart from, but within a web of interconnected lives. This is where listening becomes your most valuable tool. Engage with your supporters, beneficiaries, and team members. Hear their stories, their ideas, and their feedback. Make them feel seen and heard, for they are the most authentic ambassadors of your cause.

Create spaces—physical or digital—where your community can gather, share, and collaborate. Encourage dialogues that are inclusive and actions that are collective. Every event, newsletter, or social media post is an opportunity to reinforce the community ethos, to remind each person that they're a crucial part of the whole.

Remember, too, that a strong community looks outwards as well as in. Reach out to partner with other organizations, businesses, and initiatives. The aim is not just to expand your network but to weave a tapestry of allies, each strengthening the other. Think of your nonprofit as a node within a larger ecosystem, thriving through cooperation and mutual support.

Cultivating a community also means celebrating together. Share your successes and acknowledge your setbacks. Be transparent about your journey. Let your community revel in the triumphs and learn from the challenges. This builds trust and a sense of ownership—your victories are their victories, and every hurdle is a chance to come together and find a way over it.

And in the quiet moments, reflect on the individual faces that make up the crowd. Personalize your gratitude. Tailor your communications. The handwritten note, the personalized email, the acknowledgment of an individual's contribution—these small gestures can have an outsized impact on someone's connection to your cause.

Above all, be consistent. Community isn't built overnight. It requires ongoing effort, a steady stream of engagement, and a commitment to cultivating relationships even when the immediate returns aren't visible. It's a long-term investment that pays dividends in loyalty, support, and the collective power to enact real, lasting change.

Your nonprofit's community is its greatest asset. Cultivate it with care, sow the seeds of partnership, and watch as the garden you tend grows into a movement capable of transforming the very landscape you work within.

Chapter 36
Teach as You Learn

Nonprofit work is as much about education as it is about service. Every challenge you encounter and every bit of knowledge you gain is not just a step forward for your team, but also a valuable lesson that can empower others. That's why the most impactful nonprofits embrace the principle of teaching as they learn.

The journey of a nonprofit is a continuous loop of learning, applying, and sharing knowledge. When you adopt a new approach or overcome a new obstacle, don't just move on to the next challenge. Pause and package that experience into a learning opportunity for your community, stakeholders, and peers.

You don't have to wait until you're an expert. The 'learning out loud' approach can be incredibly powerful. It demystifies the process of trial and error and shows that growth is often non-linear and fraught with setbacks. This transparency not only humanizes your organization but also inspires others to pursue their own paths of discovery and change.

Conduct workshops, write blog posts, host webinars, or simply have one-on-one conversations. Use these as platforms to share what's working and what isn't. The lessons you share will ripple outwards, helping to elevate the entire nonprofit sector. Your fresh insights can spark innovation, prevent others from repeating mistakes, and build collective wisdom.

In this sharing, there's also a reciprocal benefit. As you teach, you often get a clearer understanding of what you know. The questions from your audience can illuminate aspects you hadn't considered, leading to new insights. Furthermore, teaching establishes you as a thought leader in your field, someone who is not only making a difference but also shaping the discourse around how to make that difference.

Remember, teaching as you learn is not about having all the answers; it's about being open to questions. It's about making the process of learning and improving as much a part of your mission as the outcomes you seek. It's about recognizing that in the world of nonprofits, knowledge shared is impact amplified.

And so, as your nonprofit moves forward, make teaching an integral part of your work. Each lesson learned is a seed planted in the fertile soil of collective progress. By teaching as you learn, you're not just building a better nonprofit, you're contributing to a smarter, more effective sector capable of creating the change we all wish to see in the world.

Chapter 37
Share Your Recipes for Change

In the nonprofit world, the secret sauce shouldn't be a secret. Your methods for creating change are as important as the outcomes. There's immense power in open-source philanthropy—sharing your "recipes" for social change can catalyze progress across the entire sector.

Imagine if every nonprofit guarded its strategies for fundraising, advocacy, or volunteer engagement as trade secrets. The sector would move at a glacial pace, reinventing the wheel in silos rather than building on a shared foundation of knowledge. That's why it's crucial to not just share your successes, but the processes and methods that led to them.

Your "recipes" could be anything from your approach to community organizing, your framework for measuring impact, or your strategy for engaging with stakeholders. These are the insights that can transform another organization's efforts from good to great. By sharing these, you help weave a tapestry of wisdom that others can draw from, enhancing the collective impact of nonprofits.

When you share your recipes for change, you invite collaboration and innovation. Others can take your ideas and adapt them, creating variations that suit their unique challenges and goals. This collaborative spirit is what drives the nonprofit sector forward, encouraging a marketplace of ideas where the best solutions are those that are continuously refined by diverse perspectives.

Moreover, sharing your methodologies can lead to unexpected partnerships and support. A donor might be inspired by your approach and choose to invest, or a volunteer might offer skills that help refine your strategy. Sharing openly communicates confidence in your mission and a commitment to community over competition.

So, open your organizational cookbook. Blog about your program design. Release white papers on your research findings. Host seminars about your intervention models. Each of these actions plants seeds for a garden of change, nurtured by the many hands of those who share your commitment to making a difference.

In the end, your legacy as a nonprofit will not only be the change you've directly enacted but also the change you've inspired by freely offering your recipes for a better world.

Chapter 38
The Impact of Transparency

In a landscape saturated with causes vying for attention and support, transparency isn't just a buzzword—it's the cornerstone of trust and authenticity. For nonprofits, being transparent means more than just financial disclosure; it means clarity of mission, openness about challenges, and honesty about impact.

Transparency starts with the simple truth that there's no shame in imperfection. Nonprofits face complex, often systemic issues, and the road to resolution is rarely straightforward. By being open about setbacks and learnings, you demonstrate a commitment to integrity that resonates with supporters. It's about showing your work—letting donors, volunteers, and the communities you serve see the effort and dedication behind the results.

This approach invites your audience to join you on your journey, cultivating a deeper engagement. It forges a bond that goes beyond transactional interactions to build a community invested in your cause. When people see the real challenges and the strategic pivots you make to address them, they understand the magnitude of the problem and the value of their support.

Moreover, transparency is a catalyst for efficacy. It drives organizations to stay true to their mission and accountable for their goals. It's a self-imposed check that aligns daily actions with long-term vision. And in a space where data and outcomes are increasingly vital, a transparent approach also ensures that your metrics of success are clear and measurable.

In practice, transparency can take many forms—from detailed annual reports to regular project updates that highlight both triumphs and trials. It's about communicating in a way that's accessible and understandable, without jargon or embellishment. It's acknowledging that every contribution, whether it be time, expertise, or funding, is integral to the mission, and that everyone deserves to know how it's being utilized.

Ultimately, the impact of transparency is twofold: it not only strengthens the trust and commitment of your existing supporters but also sets a standard that elevates the entire nonprofit sector. It fosters an environment where success is shared, and setbacks are seen as stepping stones rather than stigmas. Through transparency, your nonprofit doesn't just stand for a cause; it stands as a beacon of trustworthiness and a paragon of principled action.

Chapter 39
Authenticity Over Aesthetics

In the clamor to stand out, nonprofits can get caught up in the aesthetics of their cause—slick marketing campaigns, flashy fundraisers, glossy brochures. But when the sheen fades, it's authenticity that endures, that inspires action and fosters long-term loyalty.

Authenticity means aligning every message and every medium with the core truths of your mission. It's a refusal to compromise on the values that constitute the heart of your organization. Your community isn't just looking for a well-designed logo or an eloquent tagline; they seek a genuine narrative that resonates with their personal convictions.

Consider the story you're telling. Is it clothed in unattainable promises or does it reflect the real, on-the-ground work being done? Authentic stories don't require a filter; they're impactful in their raw form. They speak of the volunteer's dedication, the beneficiary's journey, the collective struggle, and the incremental victories along the way.

This authenticity forges a stronger, more personal connection than any aesthetic could. It invites supporters into the fold not as spectators but as partners. It's about showing the human side of your nonprofit—the faces, the stories, the passion that fuels the cause. When the veneer is stripped away, what's left is the authentic pulse of a mission that lives and breathes through its community.

Furthermore, authenticity breeds innovation. When you're true to your mission, you open the door to creative solutions that aesthetics alone could never achieve. You allow the unique challenges of your cause to dictate original strategies, rather than letting the allure of a well-trodden path stifle your approach.

Putting authenticity at the forefront doesn't mean neglecting the visual aspect of your brand; it means ensuring that every visual element communicates something true about your cause. It's a commitment to substance, to making sure that when someone scratches the surface, they find something real and engaging beneath.

In the end, the choice between authenticity and aesthetics is a choice between enduring substance and fleeting charm. One builds a foundation of trust and respect, the other risks crumbling under scrutiny. As you build your nonprofit's narrative, let authenticity be your guide. It's the only way to ensure that your story not only captivates but also compels genuine engagement and sustainable support.

Part 6
Team Building

Chapter 40
Recruit for Necessity, Not Luxury

In the world of nonprofits, each new hire must be a linchpin, an essential part of the machine that propels the mission forward. This isn't the realm of corporate excess where roles may be created as a luxury. Here, every role is a necessity.

Recruitment, therefore, is not about padding your organization with redundancies but about filling gaps that are critical to your cause. It's about discerning the difference between the nice-to-haves and the must-haves. Each person you bring aboard should provide a skill, a perspective, or a drive that your nonprofit is actively missing, something that turns the gears of progress faster and more efficiently.

Ask yourself: Does this role amplify our ability to make an impact? If the answer isn't a resounding yes, then it's time to reevaluate the necessity of the position.

Recruiting for necessity means taking a hard look at your organizational strategy and identifying the places where an extra hand will make the difference between stagnation and advancement. It's about recognizing that while volunteers are the lifeblood of many nonprofits, there are certain skills and tasks that require the commitment and expertise of a paid position.

It's also about understanding that the allure of a larger staff is often just vanity metrics—a way to make the organization seem bigger, perhaps more influential, but not necessarily more effective. The true measure of your nonprofit's influence is not in the number of its employees but in the efficacy of its actions.

When you do recruit, seek out individuals who are not only skilled but also deeply aligned with your mission. You need people who are willing to roll up their sleeves and tackle the nitty-gritty, who find satisfaction not in a title or a corner office but in the real, measurable change they're a part of.

These recruits will be your mission's champions—they're in it for the cause, not the accolades. They'll be the ones who stay late not because they have to, but because they believe in the work. They'll bring ideas and energy to the table, not because it's expected, but because they can't imagine doing anything less.

In the end, recruiting for necessity is about quality over quantity. It's about building a team that's lean, passionate, and immensely effective—a team that embodies the adage, "If you want to go fast, go alone; if you want to go far, go together." In the journey for change, these are the companions you need: necessary, not luxury.

Chapter 41
The Right Person, Not Just Any Person

In the heartbeat of every successful nonprofit lies a team that doesn't just function; it thrives on shared passion and commitment. The recruitment mantra here is clear: hire the right person, not just any person. This approach isn't a luxury—it's a necessity for creating real, enduring change.

Nonprofits face unique challenges, and they require a special breed of individual to navigate these waters—a blend of idealist and realist, someone who dreams of what could be but understands the hard work needed to make it happen. They must be innovators, collaborators, and above all, believers in your cause.

But how do you recognize the right person? They are the ones who can articulate not just what your mission means to them, but how they see themselves contributing to it. They don't just fit into your organization's culture—they enrich it. They are the ones who look beyond the job description and see the bigger picture, who find motivation not in the paycheck but in the progress they are part of.

The right person brings more than skills; they bring a spark. They are eager to learn and even more eager to apply that knowledge. They don't shy away from the trenches; they lead the charge, inspiring others with their dedication.

Making the mistake of hiring just any person can be costly for a nonprofit. It's not just about the financial implications—it's about the momentum lost, the morale dented, and the mission diluted. But when you find the right person, they become more than an employee; they become an ally, an advocate, and a driving force for your cause.

The right person understands that success in the nonprofit

sector isn't measured in profit margins or product launches—it's measured in lives touched, communities transformed, and landscapes regenerated. They find satisfaction in the collective achievement, in knowing that their work contributes to a legacy that will outlive their own tenure.

So, when you're next looking to expand your team, pause and consider: Will this person carry the torch of our mission with the care it deserves? Will they advance our cause with integrity and ingenuity? If the answer is yes, you've found more than a candidate; you've found a crusader for your cause.

Remember, in a landscape where every decision, every hire, and every day counts towards the greater good, the right person is not just a cog in the wheel—they are the ones helping to steer it.

Chapter 42
Diverse Teams, Richer Solutions

The recipe for innovation within the nonprofit sector is unequivocal: it calls for diversity. Diversity in thoughts, experiences, backgrounds, and perspectives. The more varied the voices at the table, the richer the solutions become. This isn't just an ideal; it's a pragmatic approach to problem-solving that leverages the full spectrum of human experience.

A nonprofit thrives when it mirrors the community it serves, understanding its needs not just through data, but through the lived experiences of its team members. A diverse team challenges the echo chamber of similarity, pushing against the boundaries of 'the way we've always done it' and asking the questions no one else thought to ask.

This diversity goes beyond the typical markers of race, gender, and age—it delves into the realms of socio-economic backgrounds, education levels, abilities, and life experiences. It's about curating a team that can approach a problem from every angle, providing insights that would otherwise be missed.

But this isn't diversity for diversity's sake. This is about building a team equipped to find the best solutions and drive the mission forward in ways that are thoughtful, inclusive, and effective. It's about creating an environment where differences are not just tolerated but celebrated, where each team member's unique viewpoint is seen as a vital piece of the puzzle.

The magic happens when a team can debate, discuss, and disagree in a space that is safe and respectful. Where the friction of differing views sparks the fire of creativity and innovation. The solutions born from such a crucible are not just good—they're groundbreaking, they're empathetic, and they resonate with a wider audience because they're crafted from a broader perspective.

Nonprofits that embrace diversity in their teams are not just paying lip service to a trend. They are opening their doors to a world of potential that can only be unlocked when a multitude of voices are given the chance to sing in harmony. They're acknowledging that to solve the complex issues we face, we need all hands on deck, each with a different grip.

Diverse teams create richer solutions because they reflect the world as it truly is—varied, colorful, and full of untapped potential. In these teams, each member brings a piece of the answer with them, and it is only together that the solution becomes whole.

As you look around your nonprofit, ask yourself if the team reflects the diversity of thought and experience needed to address the issues at hand. If not, it's time to broaden your recruitment horizons. Because when you build a team with diversity at its core, you're not just solving problems—you're discovering a world of richer solutions.

Chapter 43
The Fallacy of the Perfect Resume

In the nonprofit world, we're in the business of human potential—not just human history. A perfect resume is a mirage, often hiding as much as it reveals. It's a fallacy to believe that a flawless trajectory of prestigious roles and accolades is a surefire predictor of passion, commitment, or future performance in the uniquely challenging nonprofit sector.

In pursuit of the 'ideal' candidate, we've become myopic, focusing on polished professionalism over raw potential and grit. But the very essence of nonprofit work often demands ingenuity and resilience that isn't always reflected in a series of well-trodden career steps. It's in the atypical experiences, the unconventional paths, and the so-called blemishes where we often find the most fervent advocates and the most dedicated warriors for our cause.

The individuals who have faced setbacks, who have taken the road less traveled, or who have switched lanes from the corporate fast track to the nonprofit byway often bring with them a treasure trove of skills and a fresh perspective that can't be quantified by traditional metrics. They come equipped with a deeper understanding of adaptability, a hands-on familiarity with real-world problems, and a palpable eagerness to apply themselves to meaningful work.

Consider the candidate who has experienced the very challenges your organization aims to address. They may lack the degree or the polished corporate veneer, but they understand the mission at a visceral level. They bring authenticity, empathy, and a personal narrative that can inspire donors and resonate with beneficiaries in a way that no polished professional spiel ever could.

It's time to recalibrate what we perceive as valuable on a resume. Let's weigh life experience, volunteer work, and the capacity to learn and grow as heavily as we do formal education and job titles.

The richness of someone's character, their demonstrated drive to make a difference, their tenacity in the face of adversity—these are the qualities that breathe life into a nonprofit's mission.

The next time a resume crosses your desk, look beyond the bullet points. Seek out the story between the lines—the struggles, the leaps of faith, the periods of growth. Ask yourself not if this person fits the mold, but whether they have the potential to enrich it, to stretch it, to break it, and ultimately, to redefine what success in your organization can look like.

In discarding the fallacy of the perfect resume, nonprofits can become beacons of true meritocracy. They can lead by example, showing that it's the imperfect, the mavericks, the life-long learners, and the passionately committed who often have the most to offer. These are the individuals who will stand shoulder to shoulder with you as you face the complex, messy, and deeply human challenges of nonprofit work. They are your undiscovered assets, the ones who will help write your organization's most impactful chapters.

Chapter 44
Experience Beyond Years

The currency of experience in the nonprofit sector isn't always tallied in years or delineated by the linear progression of positions. It's measured in depth, breadth, and the intensity of engagement. The most profound insights and the capacity to affect change can come from those whose years may be few, but whose experiences run deep.

In the crucible of nonprofit work, we often find that the young intern who has spent six months in the field carries insights that rival those of a seasoned desk strategist. It's the fresh eyes, the ones unclouded by 'the way it's always been done,' that spot the new pathways to impact. They are the ones who ask 'Why not?' and 'What if?' — questions that lead to innovation and breakthrough.

The mistake is to equate age with experience — to assume that the longer someone has been in the industry, the more they have to contribute. This is a fallacy that discounts the young voices who are not only our future but also our present. They are the digital natives, the social media savvies, the globally-minded and interconnected. They bring a fluency in the languages of technology, culture, and social change that is indispensable in modern nonprofit work.

On the flip side, let's not forget those who've discovered their calling to nonprofit work later in life. Their years in other sectors aren't a detour; they're a rich repository of transferable skills and diverse perspectives. Their varied experiences can inject practical wisdom and cross-disciplinary thinking into a field that greatly benefits from such cross-pollination.

Let's redefine what we mean by 'experience.' Let's value the depth of someone's encounters with the world, their personal growth, their resilience, and their capacity for empathy. Let's appreciate the breadth of their curiosity, the diversity of their interactions, and their ability to translate those into action for the greater good.

The young activist who has rallied communities, the volunteer who has dedicated countless hours to a cause, the new graduate who has researched tirelessly about an issue — their experiences are just as valid, just as rich, just as capable of advancing our mission. They remind us that age is but a number, and it's the experiences beyond those years that can fuel our collective drive for change.

Nonprofits, therefore, must not only accommodate but actively seek out this broader definition of experience. By doing so, they can build a mosaic of perspectives that reflects the very communities they aim to serve. This new vanguard of diverse, passionate contributors stands ready not to fill the shoes of those who came before them, but to walk new paths in shoes of their own making.

Chapter 45
Look Beyond Credentials

The hallmarks of a great contributor in the nonprofit sector are seldom encapsulated in a series of acronyms or credentials following a name. The heart of impactful work lies not in the letters of recommendation, but in the spirit of determination, the authenticity of passion, and the evidence of hands-on engagement with the world's pressing issues.

Credentials have their place. They can be a shorthand for a certain level of expertise, a promise of specific knowledge. But they are not the be-all and end-all. In the pursuit of change and the drive to make a difference, the nonprofit world must look beyond the traditional markers of competence and consider the unorthodox, the unconventional, the life-learnt.

The person who has lived through hardship can navigate the complexities of poverty with a nuance that no degree can confer. The volunteer who has clocked thousands of hours has a practical wisdom that you won't find in textbooks. The community organizer might lack a formal degree in social work, but they understand the rhythms and the needs of their community better than any outside expert could.

By prioritizing lived experience, demonstrable skills, and a clear commitment to the cause, nonprofits can tap into a wellspring of dedication and know-how that is often overlooked. Credentials can sometimes act as a barrier, ruling out potential game-changers who lack conventional qualifications but possess the insight, the initiative, and the drive to make a tangible difference.

The most innovative nonprofits are those that recognize potential, talent, and motivation regardless of their packaging. They're the ones that value the self-taught coder, the natural-born leader, the autodidact strategist, and the empathetic listener. They're the organizations that understand that the most impactful members of their team might come from walks of life that don't include cap and gown ceremonies.

Let's start seeing beyond the parchment and the pomp. Let's recognize the significance of real-world learning and the diversity of paths that lead to expertise. The sector needs thinkers and doers, creators and sympathizers, who come from every echelon of life, carrying their unique sets of skills and experiences.

When we look beyond credentials, we don't lower the bar — we broaden the gateway. We invite a richer, more varied set of experiences into our fold, enhancing our collective ability to address multifaceted problems with empathy, creativity, and authenticity. We foster a community of contributors who bring more than just expertise; they bring perspectives that resonate with those we aim to serve, and they remind us that at the end of the day, our mission is not to amass credentials, but to amass impact.

Part 7
Resilience

Chapter 46
When Things Go Wrong, Own It

In the relentless pursuit of social good, stumbles are inevitable. Missteps and mistakes are the unspoken verses of the nonprofit narrative. They are not, however, the death knell of a mission — unless they are met with denial and deflection. When things go awry, as they sometimes will, the mettle of a nonprofit is tested not by the error itself, but by the response it elicits.

Own it.

This is the stark, yet soulful mantra for every nonprofit. To own a mistake is not simply to admit to it. It is to embrace the inherent vulnerability of the work, to understand that fallibility is a thread in the human fabric, and to recognize that there is profound strength in transparency.

Owning a mistake means standing in front of those you serve, your team, your donors, your community, and saying, "We erred." It means laying bare the what and the why — dissecting the mistake not for self-flagellation but for learning, for growth. It is a display of respect for the cause and those committed to it, acknowledging that they deserve the truth, even when it's uncomfortable.

The fear of reputational damage often drives organizations to bury their blunders, but the nonprofit sphere, with its ethos of integrity and trust, can ill afford such subterfuge. Donors, beneficiaries, and the broader community can forgive faults, but duplicity is a harder pill to swallow.

Moreover, owning mistakes is the foundation of improvement. It's the first step toward ensuring that the same error isn't repeated, that lessons are learnt, and that systems are improved. It converts the misstep into a stepping stone, paving the way for better, stronger, more effective interventions.

It also sets a cultural cornerstone. In a space where owning mistakes is the norm, team members are not paralyzed by the fear of failure. They are emboldened to innovate, to try, to push the boundaries — because they know that if they falter, the response will be constructive, not punitive.

Owning it is more than accountability — it is an affirmation of the nonprofit's humanity. It says, "We are human. We are learning. We are growing." And in that vulnerability lies the genuine connection with others — because a nonprofit is not an entity; it is a collective of individuals striving toward a shared vision.

So, when things go wrong — and at some point, they will — own it. Do it promptly, do it clearly, and do it with the intention to mend and move forward. The integrity of your mission depends on it, and the trust of your community is fortified by it.

Chapter 47
The Speed of Response Matters

Speed can be a virtue as much as it's a necessity, especially when the unexpected occurs. In the interconnected and often unforgiving realm of public perception, the pace at which a nonprofit reacts to challenges, criticism, or crises can significantly influence the trajectory of the aftermath.

Respond swiftly.

The tempo of your response is sometimes just as critical as the response itself. It signifies attentiveness, shows competence, and demonstrates respect for the concerns at hand. When an issue emerges, it's like an open wound; the longer it remains unaddressed, the more likely it is to fester, leading to skepticism, doubt, and potentially a loss of faith among those you aim to serve and those who support you.

This is not to encourage a hasty reply that lacks substance or sincerity — that would be counterproductive. The objective is to communicate promptly that you are aware of the issue and are actively working on a resolution. It's about striking that delicate balance between the urgency of the moment and the thoroughness of your approach.

In the digital age, news spreads at the click of a button. Social media can amplify a small hiccup into a full-blown crisis if left unchecked. That's why the agility of your nonprofit's response system — how quickly you can gather the team, assess the situation, and issue a statement — can often determine how well you navigate turbulent waters.

The swift response also showcases your nonprofit's agility — your ability to pivot, to adapt, and to approach disruptions with a clear head. It's a testament to your organization's preparedness and its crisis management protocols. This does not go unnoticed.

Stakeholders, from the communities you help to the donors that fund you, value this responsiveness. It reassures them that their trust is well-placed, that their investment, whether it be time, resources, or belief, is in good hands.

In essence, the speed of your response can temper the scale of a problem. It can prevent a spark from becoming a wildfire. It's the demonstration of a proactive rather than a reactive stance. And it sets the tone for how the situation will unfold — with you at the helm, steering with confidence, or scrambling to regain control.

So, as a nonprofit leader, make haste when circumstances demand it. Let your prompt reply be the first note in the symphony of your resolution efforts. Because when it comes to addressing issues, the speed of response doesn't just matter — it's pivotal.

Chapter 48
The Art of the Genuine Apology

In the landscape of nonprofit work, mistakes are inevitable. They are the byproduct of human efforts, of risks taken, and initiatives tried. However, when errors occur, the art of apologizing becomes a critical skill. A genuine apology can mend fences, rebuild trust, and demonstrate humility.

Apologize sincerely.

A genuine apology has no room for "ifs" and "buts." It's not a vehicle for excuses or a platform to deflect blame. It's a moment of vulnerability, a clear admission that something went wrong and that you, your team, or your organization is responsible.

Begin with "I'm sorry" or "We apologize." These powerful words can disarm the most potent of critiques when said sincerely. Acknowledge the specifics of what went wrong — this shows that you understand the issue and its impact. It's a critical step towards rebuilding trust.

It's not enough to simply express regret; you must also take responsibility. An apology that shifts blame or minimizes the issue is worse than no apology at all. It can come off as disingenuous, exacerbating the situation. Take ownership of the mistake, for it's in the act of owning up to errors that integrity shines through.

Then, discuss the path forward. What are the steps being taken to ensure the mistake doesn't happen again? How will you rectify the situation? A plan of action signifies that your apology isn't empty — that it's the beginning of a solution, not the end of an acknowledgment.

Reflect on the emotions involved. Whether it's disappointment, frustration, or hurt, show that you understand and care about the feelings of those affected. Empathy can be as crucial as the solution itself because it connects on a human level, reminding those involved that at the heart of your nonprofit are people — caring, dedicated, and fallible.

Remember, timing is crucial. Delayed apologies can lose their effectiveness. Address the issue as soon as you fully understand what went wrong and the extent of the impact. This timeliness shows that you prioritize the concerns and wellbeing of those impacted over the comfort of your organization.

The art of apologizing is not just about saying "sorry." It's about authenticity, accountability, and action. A well-crafted apology respects the intelligence and the feelings of your audience, and it reinforces your commitment to your nonprofit's values and mission.

In the end, the genuine apology is about restoring faith. It's an open door after a stumble, an invitation to watch you improve and an opportunity to emerge stronger, more connected, and more committed than before.

Chapter 49
Frontline Empathy

Empathy is the cornerstone of impactful nonprofit work. It's not just about understanding the statistics and facts surrounding a cause; it's about connecting with the heartbeats behind them. Frontline empathy means going beyond observing from a distance — it involves immersing oneself in the reality of those you're striving to help.

For a nonprofit leader, frontline empathy requires you to step out from behind your desk and stand alongside those at the heart of your mission. It means listening to their stories, understanding their challenges firsthand, and feeling the texture of their daily lives.

This isn't just about building rapport; it's about ensuring that the solutions you create are not just well-intended, but well-informed and practical. When you experience the ground reality, the impact of what you do becomes more tangible in your mind, and therefore, in your organization's actions.

Encourage your team to do the same. When the entire organization operates with a frontline perspective, your approach shifts. You move away from abstract notions of aid and support, and toward genuine, human-centered service.

Frontline empathy also breaks down the us-versus-them mentality that can inadvertently arise in nonprofit work. When you stand in the shoes of those you serve, they cease to be just beneficiaries; they become partners in the journey towards a better situation, a better life.

This practice isn't without its emotional cost. It can be challenging and draining. You'll be touched by stories of hardship and resilience that may weigh heavy on your heart. It's crucial to balance this empathy with self-care and support within your team, ensuring that while your hearts are in the field, you have a network to sustain your spirits.

In your communications, let this frontline empathy be evident. Share the stories that moved you, the situations that challenged you, and how these experiences are shaping the work you do. This transparency builds trust and invites your community to not just sympathize, but empathize alongside you.

Frontline empathy isn't a tactic; it's a commitment to seeing, feeling, and serving from the heart of the matter. It's about letting those experiences shape your work, so that every decision made and every dollar spent is a true reflection of the needs and hopes of those you serve.

In conclusion, frontline empathy isn't just good practice, it's essential. It reinforces your mission's relevance and urgency, it grounds your strategies in reality, and it connects your work to the very souls you're working for. It's here, in the cradle of human connection, that nonprofits find their strongest voice and their deepest impact.

Chapter 50
Take a Breath Before Responding

In the fast-paced world of nonprofits, where every decision can feel urgent, it's easy to fall into the trap of instant reactions. But here's a counterintuitive truth: the most effective response often comes from a moment of pause. Before hitting 'send,' signing off on a project, or navigating a conflict, take a breath. That breath is where clarity is found, and sometimes, where crises are averted.

This isn't about delaying action; it's about ensuring your actions are considered and reflect your nonprofit's values and mission. It's about responding, not reacting. A reaction is immediate, driven by the emotions of the moment. A response is thoughtful, taking into account the larger picture and the potential ripple effects of your words and decisions.

Teach your team this art of the intentional pause. Encourage a culture where a moment of collected thought is respected, not rushed through. Whether it's a tough email, a funding challenge, or a project setback, the space created by a breath can change the outcome from one of tension to one of understanding.

This principle extends to every layer of your organization. When planning a campaign, take a breath and ask if it aligns with your core objectives. When dealing with donors, pause to ensure that their vision is in harmony with your mission. And when managing volunteers, remember that a breath can give you the patience to see their potential, not just their immediate output.

In personal interactions, this pause is just as vital. It's in this space that empathy grows. By not jumping to conclusions or speaking from a place of frustration, you open up the possibility for more compassionate communication. This isn't only about being kinder—it's about being more effective. People respond to understanding, and they commit to causes where they feel heard and valued.

The pause can also be a tool for innovation. It allows you to step back from the 'way we've always done things' and ask if there's a better approach. It might be just the moment needed for a new, revolutionary idea to take root—one that could propel your cause forward in ways you hadn't imagined.

Finally, use the breath as a checkpoint for integrity. Before making commitments or launching initiatives, ensure they're true to the essence of what your nonprofit stands for. Misalignments can be costly, not just in resources, but in credibility.

In your next moment of decision or discussion, remember: Take a breath. It's a simple act, but within it lies the wisdom of better decisions, stronger relationships, and a more impactful nonprofit presence.

Part 8
Values

Chapter 51
Culture is Lived, Not Imposed

Culture in a nonprofit isn't built by dictating it; it's cultivated through daily actions. It's what happens when the strategic plan closes and real life opens. It's the unwritten rules that guide behavior when nobody's looking. If you want a culture of innovation, your team needs to see you innovate. If you desire a culture of transparency, your books and decisions must be open. You can't just claim values; you have to live them, celebrate them, and sometimes, make the hard choices to defend them.

When it comes to creating a thriving nonprofit culture, edicts from on high don't hold much water. What does make a difference is leadership by example. People will follow where you lead, not because they have to, but because they believe in the authenticity of your actions. This means being the first to admit mistakes, to embrace change, and to throw yourself into the work alongside everyone else.

A positive, impactful culture grows from what you reward, what you tolerate, and what you refuse to accept. It's easy to say you value 'innovation,' but do you reward the tried and true over the bold new idea? Do you tolerate fear of failure, or do you treat it as a learning opportunity? Do you refuse to accept that 'we've always done it this way' as an answer? These are the daily decisions that shape the true culture of your nonprofit.

Remember, a strong culture often means a diverse culture, one that brings together a variety of perspectives, experiences, and ideas. It means creating an environment where difference is not just tolerated, but welcomed and leveraged for the greater good of your mission. This doesn't happen overnight, and it certainly doesn't happen through mandates. It happens through a consistent, daily commitment to the values you espouse.

Moreover, the right culture has a ripple effect. It goes beyond the walls of your office and extends into the community you serve. It's reflected in the respect you show to those you're helping, in the integrity of your programs, and in the transparency of your results. Your culture becomes your brand, an identity that speaks volumes before you even make the ask for support.

And when challenges arise, as they inevitably do, it's the lived culture that will hold your nonprofit together. A strong culture provides a foundation that can weather the tough times. It's the trust that's been built, the resilience that's been fostered, and the shared vision that everyone is working towards.

In every meeting, every fundraiser, every program, let your culture be lived, not just spoken of. Let it be the heart of your nonprofit, palpable in every action and decision. When your culture is lived, it becomes your most powerful advocate, your guide, and the hallmark of your impact.

Chapter 52
Fluid Decisions for a Stable Mission

A nonprofit's mission is its anchor, holding steadfast amid the changing tides of the sector. Yet, while the mission must remain stable, the decisions around how to achieve it must remain fluid. In the nonprofit world, rigidity can be the enemy of progress. The landscape is ever-evolving – funding sources, community needs, policy changes – and organizations must be adept at navigating these waters with agile decision-making.

Fluidity in decision-making doesn't imply a lack of direction; it means being adaptable in your approach while keeping your eyes fixed on the mission's horizon. It's about having a plan but being prepared to pivot when external circumstances or new information dictate. This agility allows a nonprofit to seize opportunities that align with its mission, even if they weren't part of the original plan.

Being fluid also means embracing experimentation. It means trying new fundraising strategies, program models, or partnership structures, evaluating their impact, and adjusting accordingly. It's not about chasing every new trend but about being discerning and willing to adjust your sails when it serves your mission.

The reality is that nonprofits operate in a world of complexity. What worked yesterday may not work tomorrow, and what works for one organization may not work for another. Fluid decision-making respects this complexity and rejects one-size-fits-all solutions. It encourages leaders to ask, "What is the best way to achieve our mission under these specific circumstances?" rather than, "How do we replicate what everyone else is doing?"

Moreover, fluid decision-making fosters a culture of inclusivity and diversity of thought. It invites input from all levels of the organization and values different perspectives. This collective approach doesn't just lead to better decisions; it also builds a stronger, more invested team. When people feel their ideas are valued, they're more committed to the mission and to finding innovative ways to advance it.

Yet, even with fluid decisions, accountability and evaluation are paramount. Each decision, while adaptable, must be made with intention and based on data, experience, and the predicted impact on the mission. And once made, each decision must be measured: Did it advance the mission? What did we learn? What will we do differently next time?

In the end, fluid decision-making is about stewardship. It's a commitment to the responsible management of resources, opportunities, and challenges with a focus on the ultimate goal – the mission. It's knowing when to stay the course and when to navigate new paths. It's how nonprofits remain resilient and relevant in a changing world.

By embracing fluidity in your decisions, your nonprofit can not only survive but thrive, moving confidently toward its mission, no matter the shifting winds of the sector.

Chapter 53
Beyond Rock Stars and Heroes

In the narrative of change, nonprofits have often sought their heroes – the standout rock stars who can rally the troops and make a splash in the media. It's a compelling story: one person or group, against the odds, achieving monumental change. However, that story is evolving. The sector is increasingly recognizing that sustainable impact requires more than just singular heroes; it requires collective effort and community engagement.

Nonprofits are not rock bands centered around a single frontman; they're orchestras where every instrument contributes to the harmony. The myth of the lone hero undermines the very essence of nonprofit work, which is collaborative and systemic change. The fixation on finding or being the rock star can overshadow the importance of team dynamics, shared leadership, and the diverse contributions that are the lifeblood of any effective organization.

This shift in perspective starts with recognizing that heroics are not scalable, and rock stars don't always make the best leaders. What happens when that one person leaves? Does the organization's impact fade away? Sustainable nonprofits build systems and cultivate a culture that outlasts any individual. They invest in the collective power of their teams, understanding that each member brings unique strengths that are critical to the mission.

It also means rethinking recognition. Celebrating the contributions of all, rather than elevating a select few, encourages a sense of ownership and investment in the mission. It means embracing humility and understanding that behind every public win are countless unseen hours of teamwork. The stories we tell should reflect this reality, giving voice to the many rather than the few.

Inclusivity also plays a crucial role in moving beyond the hero complex. By creating space for diverse voices and democratizing the idea of leadership within the organization, nonprofits ensure that they are not just being led, but are being steered by a community of individuals who are all leaders in their own right.

The most successful nonprofits are those that build resilience not on individual heroism, but on collective effort. They understand that change is a chorus, not a solo performance. It's about creating a culture where every staff member, volunteer, and stakeholder feels like they are part of something bigger, something that doesn't hinge on a singular identity.

This chapter doesn't negate the impact of inspiring leaders; rather, it emphasizes that the true measure of an organization's strength is not in its figureheads, but in its foundations – the people at all levels who commit themselves to the mission every day. The shift from heroism to collective empowerment is not just a change in strategy; it's a transformation in ethos.

Nonprofits must continue to evolve beyond the allure of rock stars and heroes and step into a narrative that celebrates collective impact – because when everyone plays a part, the whole organization, and its mission, shines brighter.

Chapter 54
Respect is Non-Negotiable

In the bustling world of nonprofits, amidst the passion-driven work and the relentless pursuit of mission, there remains one foundational pillar that must never crumble: respect. It's a simple yet profound principle that steers the culture of any organization towards a path of integrity and empathy. In the realm of social impact, respect is more than courtesy; it is the bedrock of partnership, collaboration, and community engagement.

This isn't just about politeness or the pleasantries exchanged over the water cooler; it's about the deep-seated recognition of every individual's inherent value and contribution. It's about listening actively, communicating openly, and valuing diverse perspectives. Whether it's between colleagues, towards volunteers, or in engagement with the communities served, respect is the thread that weaves a tapestry of trust and mutual understanding.

For nonprofits, respect translates into several key practices. Firstly, it's about ensuring inclusivity in decision-making. It means that whether it's a staff member, a donor, or a beneficiary, everyone's voice has weight and is considered with seriousness. When individuals feel respected, they are more likely to invest themselves fully in the mission of the organization.

Secondly, respect is about transparency. It is a commitment to honesty in operations, in successes, and failures. This transparency builds trust not only within the organization but also with the public and the communities served. When people trust that they are getting the full picture, their respect for the organization grows.

Furthermore, respect means recognizing boundaries and valuing personal time and space. It means understanding that burnout is not a badge of honor but a warning sign that the system needs adjustment. Nonprofits that respect their employees' and volunteers' time and wellness create a healthier, more productive environment.

In a nonprofit, respect also extends beyond human interactions. It's about respecting the resources entrusted to the organization by the community and donors. It means stewarding these resources wisely, with a keen sense of responsibility and accountability.

Lastly, respect is about acknowledging the dignity and autonomy of those being served. It is steering clear of paternalistic attitudes and instead, partnering with communities. It's about empowering individuals rather than dictating solutions, recognizing that those who live the challenges every day are the most knowledgeable about effective solutions.

In every chapter of a nonprofit's story, respect must be a constant character. It's what allows the organization to navigate challenges with grace, to grow without losing its core values, and to impact without overstepping. When respect is non-negotiable, it creates an environment where everyone — from the CEO to the newest volunteer — feels valued and driven by a shared mission.

For any nonprofit looking to forge a legacy that lasts, to create change that truly resonates, and to build a community that stands strong, it all starts with respect. Because when respect is given freely and integrated into the fabric of an organization, the potential for genuine, transformative impact is boundless.

Chapter 55
Encourage Life Beyond Work

For nonprofits, where the work is often deeply personal and the stakes are high, the lines between professional and personal life can become blurred. However, an organization that wants to flourish must acknowledge and embrace the world that exists beyond its mission — the world where its people lead full and varied lives. It is essential for nonprofits to encourage a life beyond work, not just as a nod to work-life balance, but as a strategy for sustainability and success.

Life beyond work means recognizing that the passion which fuels the fight for any cause is the same passion that fills one's life with hobbies, family, and adventures. These activities recharge the soul and bring fresh perspectives to daunting challenges. When nonprofits celebrate and encourage these pursuits, they acknowledge the wholeness of their teams and, by extension, increase their organization's resilience.

This isn't just about taking vacation days or stepping out early to catch a child's soccer game — though these are important. It's about creating an organizational culture that sees value in employees who are rested, well-rounded, and connected to their communities. It's about understanding that time spent away from the desk is not time lost but invested in the well-being and long-term productivity of the team.

In practice, encouraging life beyond work can take many forms. It could be as straightforward as setting and respecting boundaries for work hours and communications. It ensures that staff do not feel compelled to answer emails late at night or during weekends, allowing them to fully disconnect and rejuvenate.

Furthermore, it could mean providing opportunities for personal development that are not limited to professional skills. Workshops on creative writing, yoga classes, or group outings to cultural events can stimulate the mind and foster team connections in a context that isn't centred on work-related stress.

Nonprofits that encourage life beyond work also often adopt flexible work arrangements. Recognizing that peak productivity does not always fit within the traditional nine-to-five framework, they allow for varied schedules that accommodate the diverse life commitments of their employees.

There is also a deeper level of support that can be provided — one that involves actively encouraging staff to pursue their passions and interests. This could be through sabbaticals, volunteer days, or even supporting a team member's side project that aligns with the organization's values. Such actions send a powerful message: that the nonprofit values its employees as complete individuals, not just as workers.

In conclusion, by encouraging a life beyond work, nonprofits don't detract from their mission; they enhance it. They build teams that are more creative, more committed, and more capable of handling the complex tasks at hand. They show that while the work they do is vital, they also understand that a single thread cannot hold the weight of the world — it takes the strength of a full tapestry, woven with diverse and rich experiences, to truly make a difference.

Chapter 56
First Mistakes Aren't Failures

In the landscape of nonprofits, the word 'mistake' often comes loaded with negative connotations of inefficiency and waste. But it's crucial to shift this perception and understand that first mistakes are not failures, but fertile ground for growth and learning.

Nonprofits are tasked with tackling some of society's most pressing issues—tasks that are inherently complex and fraught with uncertainty. When the path forward is uncharted, missteps are not just inevitable; they are necessary. It is through these initial stumbles that organizations learn what works and, just as importantly, what doesn't.

Reframing the narrative around mistakes starts at the top. Leadership within a nonprofit must foster a culture where taking calculated risks is encouraged, and where the inevitable mistakes that arise from those risks are treated as opportunities for learning rather than occasions for censure. It is a shift from a fixed mindset, where abilities are set in stone and mistakes are seen as character flaws, to a growth mindset that values development and progress.

This doesn't mean operating recklessly under the guise of innovation, but rather approaching new initiatives with a strategy that allows for testing and iteration. When a new program or campaign is being developed, it's essential to set benchmarks for success, but also to plan for feedback loops that can catch missteps early and redirect efforts efficiently.

First mistakes made in the spirit of exploration and progress can be invaluable. They serve as guideposts, helping to clarify objectives and refine tactics. When a fundraising event fails to meet its target, the lessons learned in that process about audience engagement and messaging can inform more successful future efforts. When a community program doesn't get the uptake anticipated, understanding the reasons why can lead to a more finely tuned and impactful offering down the line.

To truly capitalize on the learning opportunities that mistakes offer, nonprofits should implement reflective practices. After-action reviews, where teams openly discuss what happened, why it happened, and how it can be done better, should be a regular feature of project cycles. This not only aids in knowledge sharing but also helps to normalize the experience of making and learning from mistakes.

Moreover, when nonprofits share their experiences of mistakes and the lessons learned with the broader sector, they contribute to a collective wisdom that can propel the entire field forward. This transparency not only benefits other organizations but also fosters trust with donors and stakeholders who appreciate the commitment to continuous improvement.

In conclusion, when nonprofits embrace first mistakes not as failures but as natural steps in the journey of making an impact, they liberate their teams from the fear of trying and failing. They build an organizational ethos that is resilient, adaptive, and ultimately more effective. By accepting mistakes as part of the narrative of progress, nonprofits can create a more forgiving and, ironically, a less fallible path to achieving their missions.

Chapter 57
Cut the Jargon

In the nonprofit world, clarity is king. Yet, far too often, organizations fall into the trap of wrapping their messages in a blanket of jargon, thinking it makes them sound more 'professional.' But here's the rub: when your language is cluttered with acronyms, buzzwords, and technical terms, your message doesn't come across as professional—it becomes inaccessible.

Jargon is the enemy of understanding. It creates barriers where there should be open doors, especially in a sector that thrives on widespread support and collective action. The aim should always be to communicate in a way that is immediately clear to anyone who stumbles upon your message, whether they're industry insiders or not.

Nonprofits need to speak the language of the people they are looking to engage—the donors, volunteers, the community, and most importantly, the people they serve. The language should be simple, direct, and free of unnecessary complexities. After all, the power of a cause is best conveyed through stories that resonate, not terminologies that require a dictionary.

Cutting the jargon does not mean diluting the message; it means distilling it to its essence. It's about getting to the heart of the matter and conveying it with the power of plain language. Consider how much more impactful it is to say, "We provide meals for children in need" instead of "We engage in nutritional provisioning for at-risk youth demographics." The first tells a story; the second reads like a line from a technical manual.

Here are a few tips for nonprofits looking to cut the jargon:

1. **Speak from the heart:** Use words that evoke emotions and paint clear pictures. Let passion lead your vocabulary choices, not the latest industry handbook.

2. **Explain concepts, don't label them:** If you must use specific terms, ensure you explain them. Make it a habit to break down concepts into relatable language.
3. **Use the grandmother test:** If you couldn't use a term or phrase when explaining your work to your grandmother (or any layperson), it's probably best to leave it out.
4. **Be specific:** Instead of saying 'capacity-building activities,' tell your audience exactly what you're doing. Are you providing training workshops? Are you offering educational resources? Be precise.
5. **Edit ruthlessly:** After drafting a piece of communication, go back through it and replace or explain any jargon that's snuck in.

By cutting the jargon, nonprofits can ensure that their messages are not only heard but felt. It's in the feeling that action takes root. Whether it's a call to donate, a request for volunteers, or an invitation to join a cause, clear, jargon-free language is what will turn passive readers into active participants in your mission. Remember, the goal is to open doors, not to put up linguistic barriers.

Chapter 58
Urgency Must Be Warranted

In the pulsing heart of a nonprofit, where every cause feels critical, the temptation to slap an 'urgent' label on every request can be overwhelming. But here's a truth that should echo through the halls of your organization: when everything is urgent, nothing is.

The power of urgency lies in its rarity. It's the nonprofit's red flashing light that says, "This is the moment. Act now!" But misuse it, and you risk numbing your audience, dulling their sense of immediacy and, ultimately, their propensity to take action.

Urgency should be reserved for those pivotal moments when the stakes are highest and the need for immediate action is real and tangible. Perhaps it's a natural disaster that requires instant humanitarian aid, or a legislative change that needs a quick rally of voices. These are the times when an urgent call makes hearts race and hands move faster.

To ensure that 'urgent' keeps its weight, here are some guidelines:

First - Save it for the critical: Before declaring something urgent, ask yourself if the situation truly requires immediate action. Will a delay result in significant harm or missed opportunity? If the answer is no, it's not urgent.

Second - Be clear about why it's urgent: When you do call on urgency, make sure you communicate why it's urgent. What are the consequences of inaction? The reason must be compelling and clear.

Third - Offer a specific action: Urgency should always be paired with a clear and actionable step. What exactly do you need your audience to do? Donate now? Sign a petition immediately? Clarity is key.

Fourth - Track your urgent appeals: Keep a log of how often

you use urgency in your communications. If you're declaring emergencies weekly, it's time to reassess.

Lastly - Follow up with outcomes: If you've sounded the alarm, let your supporters know the outcome. This builds trust and reinforces the significance of their timely actions.

The true power of urgency is not in the word itself, but in the genuine need it represents. When used judiciously, it can galvanize an audience to powerful and impactful action. But when overused, it can lead to a disengaged audience that scrolls past your pleas without a second glance.

In the end, your mission is too important to be lost in a sea of false urgency. Be strategic, be sincere, and when the time is genuinely critical, your call for urgent action will resonate deeply, spurring the kind of immediate response that can make a real difference.

Chapter 59
Authentic Voice

In a world inundated with marketing gimmicks and corporate jargon, the authentic voice of a nonprofit stands out like a beacon. It's not just a tool for communication; it's the very essence that connects the cause with the community, the donors, and the volunteers. It is the embodiment of the organization's values, mission, and vision.

An authentic voice isn't polished to an unreal sheen; it's honest, raw, and real. It speaks of the struggles just as loudly as it celebrates the victories. It tells the story of the people served, not as beneficiaries of charity, but as equals in a mission for change. This voice is not crafted in a boardroom. It's shaped on the ground, at the heart of service, and in the reflections of those who put in the work day after day.

For nonprofits, developing an authentic voice means shedding the fear of vulnerability. Sharing the challenges faced—be it a lack of resources, a program that didn't yield expected results, or a shift in strategic direction—can be daunting. Yet, this transparency breeds a deeper trust and creates a stronger connection with stakeholders who appreciate honesty over a facade of infallibility.

Leaders and communicators in the nonprofit sector must resist the urge to mimic the corporate tone of their for-profit counterparts. While professionalism is necessary, it should not come at the cost of sounding detached or impersonal. An authentic voice resonates with emotion, it carries the passion of the individuals involved, and it aligns closely with the lived experiences of the cause it champions.

Moreover, an authentic voice is inclusive. It recognizes the diversity of the community it serves and reflects it. This means not only acknowledging a range of experiences but actively involving different voices in the conversation. By doing so, a nonprofit's narrative becomes a chorus of authenticity, richer and more impactful than a single voice could ever be.

In the practical application of this voice, it's crucial for nonprofits to communicate consistently across all platforms. Whether it's through social media, newsletters, or direct engagement, the core message and tone should be unmistakable and true to the organization's identity. The authenticity of the voice is not just in what is communicated, but how it is done—always aiming to connect, engage, and inspire action.

Nonprofits also thrive when they can articulate their cause and the impact of their work without jargon or buzzwords. Simple, clear language that speaks directly to the hearts and minds of the audience is far more effective than any industry lingo. It's not about dumbing down the message; it's about elevating it to a universal level where it's accessible and engaging for everyone.

In writing the story of a nonprofit, it is the authentic voice that will endure in people's memories. It's the narrative of real change, of humanity, and of a shared vision for a better future. And it is this voice that will rally the support, galvanize the community, and incite the passion needed to drive forward even the most ambitious of missions.

Chapter 60
Begin with the Mission in Mind

The guiding star for any nonprofit organization is its mission. It's the foundational statement that declares your purpose and directs your efforts. Beginning with the mission in mind is essential not just for staying on course, but for ensuring that every strategy, project, and endeavor you undertake contributes to your ultimate goal.

In the bustling day-to-day operations, it's easy to drift away from your core mission. New opportunities arise, challenges demand attention, and before you know it, you're engaged in activities that, while worthwhile, may not align with your primary objectives. This is why it's crucial to regularly recalibrate and ask, "Does this serve our mission?"

Starting with the mission in mind also means that every new idea is evaluated based on how well it serves your central purpose. It's a litmus test that can simplify decision-making. When faced with multiple paths, choose the one that most directly advances your mission. This focus prevents mission creep and keeps resources concentrated on impact.

Moreover, beginning with the mission in mind isn't just for the leadership team; it's a principle that should permeate every level of the organization. When every volunteer, staff member, and partner understands and embraces the mission, their collective efforts create a powerful synergy that propels the organization forward.

This principle also has external implications. When your constituents, donors, and the broader community see a nonprofit consistently acting in harmony with its mission, trust is built. A strong, mission-driven reputation makes your organization a reliable and credible actor in the nonprofit space. This trust is essential for cultivating long-term relationships and securing the resources necessary for sustaining and expanding your work.

But how do you keep the mission front and center? Make it visible. Literally. Display your mission statement prominently in your office, on your website, and in your communications. Encourage discussions about the mission in meetings and check-ins. And celebrate when projects or initiatives fully embody the mission – let success stories serve as exemplars for mission-centric efforts.

Beginning with the mission in mind also means being willing to say no. Some projects, partnerships, or funding opportunities may be enticing, but if they don't advance your mission, they can dilute your organization's effectiveness. The discipline to turn down such opportunities can be challenging, but it ensures that your nonprofit remains true to its purpose.

In a world that is complex and ever-changing, your mission is the constant that should guide every decision. It's the touchstone for measuring success and the beacon that ensures your nonprofit's journey is always moving in the right direction. Start every endeavor by asking, "How does this support our mission?" and you'll create an organization that is focused, effective, and true to its cause.

Conclusion
Forging Ahead

As we turn the final page of this journey, it's essential to take a moment to reflect on the path we've walked together. This book has been an invitation to think differently, to challenge norms, and to approach the noble endeavor of nonprofit work with a fresh, innovative perspective akin to that of the most agile startups.

The world of nonprofits is as varied and dynamic as the causes they champion. Yet, whether you're advocating for environmental protection, championing social justice, fighting hunger, or working on any other mission, there are common threads that bind all those who endeavor to make a difference: passion, purpose, and the unwavering belief that change is possible.

The insights shared within these chapters, drawn from the wellspring of collective wisdom and practical experience, are not prescriptive laws but rather guiding principles to navigate the complex, often challenging, yet deeply rewarding world of nonprofit work.

Remember, innovation isn't just for the profit-driven. It's also the heartbeat of a thriving nonprofit. Embrace creativity, foster a culture of open-mindedness, and never be afraid to take the road less traveled if it promises a better outcome for your cause.

Focus on impact over size, on being effective rather than just busy. As we've discussed, this might mean refining your mission, embracing technology, fostering diversity, or reshaping your approach to fundraising and community engagement.

Building a nonprofit is akin to steering a ship through uncharted waters. There will be storms and there will be calm seas. Your job is not to avoid all storms but to navigate through them with resilience and to keep your ship—your mission—on course.

As leaders, volunteers, staff, and supporters, we are all stewards of the missions we hold dear. The responsibility is great, but so too is the reward. When a life is changed, a community improved, or a piece of the world saved, it's a testament to your commitment and hard work.

Let's carry forward the knowledge that our efforts, grounded in sincerity and strategic thought, are more than drops in the ocean. They are the ripples that can turn into the waves of change.

So, as you close this book, don't see it as an end but as a beginning. A call to action to implement what you've learned, to inspire those around you, and to forge ahead with renewed vigor and vision.

For the work of nonprofits is never truly done. Each day presents new challenges, new opportunities to make a difference, and new frontiers to explore. Your mission matters. Your work matters. You are the architects of hope, the champions of progress, and the torchbearers for a brighter future.

Forge ahead with purpose. The world is waiting.

Acknowledgments

There is a unique joy and profound gratitude that comes with the opportunity to write these acknowledgments. This section of the book is far more than a customary nod to those who have supported me; it is a heartfelt celebration of the collective spirit that has propelled my journey.

To the thousands of nonprofits and the professionals who breathe life into them, you are the unsung heroes of our time. Your stories have been the ink in my pen, and your challenges and triumphs have shaped these pages. Your resilience, creativity, and unwavering commitment to service have not only inspired me, but have also been a beacon of hope in a world that often seems to need it most. I am deeply grateful for the knowledge shared, the inspiration given, and the support extended over the past decade.

To my parents, Berry and Judi Patrick, words seem a modest vessel to contain my gratitude. You have been the architects of my foundation, crafting it with love, support, and the kind of wisdom that only parents can provide. Without your guidance, the path of my life would be drastically different, and this book would remain unwritten.

Charlotte Gwynn, your belief in me has been both a comfort and a catalyst. You've been a constant in the tumult of ups and downs this year. Without you, this book would not have been possible. Thank you for all that you do for both me and everyone you come in contact with.

A fraternal salute to my brothers—Jacob, Justin, and Joseph Patrick. Our shared experiences are the threads from which I've woven my passion and my character. You have all, in your own unique ways, contributed to the person I have become, and for that, I am forever thankful.

Finally, I dedicate this book to my late grandfather, Dr. David Aronson. His life was a testament to the power of passion and dedication. Papa, you instilled in me the values of hard work and integrity, and your support for my career and my passions knew no bounds. Your legacy is etched not only in these pages but in the very fabric of who I am.

This book, much like the mission of every nonprofit it seeks to serve, is about hope, action, and the ripple effect of good deeds. May it honor the memory of my grandfather and the collective work of the many who strive to make a difference each day.

With the utmost gratitude,
Jordan Patrick

Made in the USA
Middletown, DE
26 October 2024